The De Forests and the Walloon Founding of New Amsterdam
◆ N ◆ E ◆ W ◆ ◆ Y ◆ O ◆ R ◆ K ◆

PRINTED PRIVATELY IN CONNECTION WITH THE CELEBRATION
OF THE THREE HUNDREDTH ANNIVERSARY OF THE
SETTLEMENT OF NEW YORK BY WALLOONS

Lucy Garrison Green

HERITAGE BOOKS
2014

HERITAGE BOOKS
AN IMPRINT OF HERITAGE BOOKS, INC.

Books, CDs, and more—Worldwide

For our listing of thousands of titles see our website
at
www.HeritageBooks.com

A Facsimile Reprint
Published 2014 by
HERITAGE BOOKS, INC.
Publishing Division
5810 Ruatan Street
Berwyn Heights, Md. 20740

Originally published:
Lincoln, Nebraska
1916

Copyright © 2003 Heritage Books, Inc.

— Publisher's Notice —
In reprints such as this, it is often not possible to remove blemishes from the original. We feel the contents of this book warrant its reissue despite these blemishes and hope you will agree and read it with pleasure.

International Standard Book Numbers
Paperbound: 978-0-7884-2336-9
Clothbound: 978-0-7884-9073-6

FOREWORD

BY a fortunate coincidence, just a short month before the celebration of the Three Hundredth Anniversary of the Settlement of New York by Walloons, this thesis was called to my attention. It was written by Miss Lucy Garrison Green of Lincoln, Nebraska, some eight years ago as qualification for her master's degree in the University of Nebraska. And it was written before any plans to celebrate this anniversary had taken shape or, so far as I know, had been considered. I found it existed only in typewritten form in the library of the University. It seemed to me to have such scholarly quality and literary charm as to merit circulation at this time. I am, therefore, having it privately printed with the consent of the writer.

I ask myself whether perhaps it does not, by its title, unduly emphasize the part which the Walloons took in the settlement of New York. There seems to be no question but that the first real settlers—those who came to stay as distinguished from those who came to trade—were "mostly Walloons." But these Walloons were sent here by the Dutch in a Dutch ship and they came from Leyden, the city of Holland which so generously befriended them, as well as their English fellow-exiles of "Mayflower" fame.

But to honor the Walloons, the descendants of those ancient Belgae who so troubled Julius Cæsar, is not less to honor the Dutch who made their enterprise possible. There is glory enough to go around. And so broad-minded a people as the Dutch certainly will not begrudge to the Walloons some of this glory.

I also question whether the title of this thesis should not have more properly been "the settlement" than "the founding" of New York. There seems to be no question but that the first permanent settlers were "mostly Walloons," who came here in 1624. There also seems to be no question but that the first organization of city government dated from 1626. But whatever distinction there may be between the word "settlement" and the word "founding" and whatever bearing that distinction may have on any anniversary date, it is 1624 that marks the three hundredth anniversary of the first Walloon emigration. Time has been too short to give the author or anyone opportunity to correct proof. Responsibility for all errors must therefore rest on the broad shoulders of the "printer's devil."

ROBERT W. DE FOREST.

April 15, 1924.

BIBLIOGRAPHY

A. Sources

1. Documents Relating to the Colonial History of the State of New York, now commonly called "New York Colonial Documents." Collected by John R. Brodhead.
   a. Holland Documents.
   b. Dutch Documents.
   c. London Documents.
2. Collections of New York Historical Society.
3. New York Colonial MSS. State Archives, Albany, N. Y.
4. Proceedings of the New York Historical Society (periodical magazine).
5. Year Books of the Holland Society of New York.
6. London Public Records.
   a. State Papers, Colonial Series, America and West Indies.
   b. British State Papers: Holland, 1622.
7. Sloane MS. 179 b. in British Museum, entitled "Journal du voyage faict par les pères de familles envoyes par Mes les Directeurs de la Compagnee des Indes Occidentales pour visiter la coste de Gujane." Written by Jesse de Forest and Jean Mousnier de la Montagne. Collected by Sir Hans Sloane, founder of the British Museum.

Bibliography

8. The New York Genealogical and Biographical Record.

9. Registers of the Huguenot Church of Sedan, translated from the French by J. W. De Forest, 1900.

10. Baptismal Register of the Walloons, Leyden. Certified copy by State Archivist, Leyden.

B. Secondary Material

1. History of the State of New York, 1853.
   JOHN ROMEYN BRODHEAD.
2. The De Forests of Avesnes and New Netherland. 1900. J. W. DE FOREST.
3. French Blood in America. 1895.
   THOMAS BALCH.
4. The American Nation: a History. 1607–1907.
   ALBERT BUSHNELL HART.
5. A Walloon Family in America. 1914.
   MRS. ROBERT W. DE FOREST.
6. History of the City of Albany. 1884.
   ARTHUR JAMES WEISE.
7. History of New Netherland, or New York under the Dutch. 1848. E. B. O'CALLAGHAN.
8. New Amsterdam and Its People. 1902.
   J. H. INNES.
9. The French in America. 1895.
   THOMAS BALCH.
10. The England and Holland of the Pilgrims. 1906. HENRY M. DEXTER and MORTON DEXTER.
11. The Puritans in Holland, England and America. 1892. DOUGLAS CAMPBELL.

THE DE FORESTS AND THE WALLOON FOUNDING OF NEW AMSTERDAM

OUTLINE

I. Introduction.
   A. Common acceptance of the Dutch as the first settlers of New Amsterdam.
   B. Casual mention of a few Walloons as included among these early Dutch settlers.
   C. Recent establishment of the fact that the De Forest colony of Walloons were predecessors of the Dutch.
II. Walloons in general.
   A. Racial history and distribution.
   B. Characteristics.
   C. Religion.
   D. Emigration due to persecution.
      1. Number migrating.
      2. Havens found.
      3. Reasons for migrating again.
      4. General Results—permanent loss to land left, gain to land sought.
III. Comparison of the Walloon Colony in Leyden with the contemporary Puritan Colony from England in Leyden.

The De Forests and the
- A. Previous experience of each colony.
- B. Fellowship in Leyden.
- C. Emigration of part of the Separatist Church under Robinson in Leyden to America in 1620.
- D. Stimulus to emigration of Walloons.

IV. Jesse De Forest, Leader of the Walloon migration to New Netherland.
- A. French origin and early connections.
- B. Family migration to Holland.
- C. Reasons leading to emigration.

V. Efforts of De Forest to arrange for the emigration of a colony under auspices of the British Virginia Company.
- A. Interview with Sir Dudley Carleton, British Ambassador to the Netherlands.
- B. Written Transactions.
  1. "The Demands" of the colonists.
  2. "The Round Robin."
  3. Reply of the Directors.
- C. Result on plans of the Walloons.

VI. Efforts of De Forest to arrange for the emigration of a colony under Dutch auspices.
- A. Petition to "The States of Holland and West Friesland" (provincial legislature).
- B. Petition to "The States General" (national legislative body of The United Netherlands).
- C. Dealings with the newly created Dutch West India Company.

Walloon Founding of New Amsterdam

VII. De Forest's Expedition to Guiana under the Dutch West India Company.
    A. General stage of colonization in South America.
    B. Sailing routes to the New World.
    C. John De Laet's "History of the New World," and Wassenaer's "Historical Account."
    D. The Journal of Jesse De Forest, Sloane MS. 179 b. "A Voyage to Guiana."
    E. "Les pères de familles": personnel of De Forest's colonists aboard the "Pigeon."
    F. Companion voyage of "The Mackerel" and "The Pigeon" from Leyden to the New World.
    G. The settlement along the Wyapoko on the Wild Coast.
    H. Death of Jesse De Forest.
    I. The colonists' return to Holland.

VIII. De Forest's contemporary Walloon colony for the Hudson River.
    A. The "Nieuwe Nederlandt," skipper Cornelis Mey; date of voyage.
    B. Personnel of the Colony.
    C. Landing on Manhattan; first experiences.
    D. Comparative historic importance of the little settlement.

IX. Expedition of Jean La Montagne, De Forest's colleague and son-in-law, to Tobago.
    A. La Montagne's return from the Guiana venture, and marriage to Rachel De Forest.

The De Forests and the
  B. Unsuccessful colony at Tobago.
  C. La Montagne's return, and readiness for new ventures.
X. Emigration of Jesse De Forest's three children, Hendrick, Isaac and Rachel, with the latter's husband, La Montagne.
  A. Gerard De Forest, brother of Jesse.
  B. Hendrick De Forest, son of Jesse.
  C. The Patroon Kiliaen van Rensselaer.
  D. The Swanendael Colony.
  E. The Rensselaerswyck Expedition.
    1. Contract between Kiliaen van Rensselaer and Gerard De Forest for joint equipment and profits of the vessel "Rensselaerswyck."
    2. Personnel of the expedition.
    3. Voyage and Landing.
  F. Location of lands first held by the De Forests.
  G. Death of Hendrick De Forest.
XI. The "Muscoota Bouweries," or Walloon homesteads.
  A. Hendrick De Forest's, afterwards Dr. La Montagne's, called "Vredendael."
  B. Isaac De Forest's, "on the Kill that runs round the Island."
  C. Philippe Du Trieux', on the East River overlooking Smit's Vly, now Fulton Market.
  D. General Conditions.
    1. Degree of comfort in home.

Walloon Founding of New Amsterdam

    2. Results of French skill and taste.
    3. Difficulty regarding service.
  E. Danger from the Indians.
    1. Leadership of La Montagne.
    2. Appeal to the West India Company.
    3. Appeal to the States General at the Hague.
    4. Later Services of La Montagne.
XII. Place held by the Walloons in the early years of New Amsterdam.
  A. Civic Organization.
    1. The Director-General.
    2. "The Nine Men."
    3. Great and Small Burghers.
    4. Minor offices.
  B. Representative Walloon Citizens.
    1. Peter Minuit.
    2. Isaac De Forest.
    3. Jean Mousnier La Montagne.
    4. Philippe Du Trieux.
  C. Descendants.
  D. Interesting contributions to the earliest life of the colony.
    1. The driving out by De Forest's Protestant Walloon colony, on their arrival in the "Nieuwe Nederlandt, in 1623-4, of the French Catholic commander about to land on Manhattan for the purpose of setting up the arms of France, then a Roman Catholic power.
    2. Establishment, by this same French-speaking, Protestant band, of the first perma-

nent town-building, crop-raising settlement of New York, never since destroyed or abandoned.

3. Purchase of the island of Manhattan from the Indians by Peter Minuit soon after his arrival in 1626.

4. Treaty of La Montagne with the sachems for the purchase of all the territory on the Schuylkill.

5. Successful defense against the Indians, at a critical time, after many massacres, by a combined force of Dutch, Walloons and English, under chief command of La Montagne.

XIII. Conclusion: Investigation of the facts by the Holland Society of New York.

A. Value to history of original sources either long overlooked or only recently available.

B. Larger share of credit, than has commonly been awarded, due to earliest Walloon settlers.

C. Recognition of Jesse De Forest as the real founder of New Amsterdam, now the City of New York.

# THE DE FORESTS AND
THE WALLOON FOUNDING
OF
NEW AMSTERDAM

Walloon Founding of New Amsterdam

THE DE FORESTS AND THE WALLOON FOUNDING OF NEW AMSTERDAM

I. INTRODUCTION

IN Brodhead's "History of the State of New York,"[1] published as long ago as 1853, but from its careful scholarship still substantially reliable, is to be found an account—fairly correct in most particulars, so far as it goes—of the Walloon colony which formed the first permanent settlement upon the island of Manhattan. In the production of this work, at a time when American research was in its infancy—as the author himself[2] says, "under the recent impulse to historical investigation"—Mr. Brodhead, with patience and conscientiousness, consulted such original authorities as were then within reach. Realizing the importance of the field, he continued, after the completion of his "History," to devote his scholarship for many years to the collection, in France, England, Holland, and America, of "Documents relating to the Colonial History of the State of New York." These papers, of great and increasing value, are now to be found in state and historical libraries under the title of "New York Colonial Documents." They comprise a variety of sources. Several of these, such as the "Holland Documents" and "Dutch Documents," are among the source-material consulted in the preparation of this paper.

[1] "History of the State of New York," by John R. Brodhead. N. Y. 1853, Ch. V, pp. 146-154.   [2] Preface to above.

The De Forests and the

While much new matter of interest in this field has since come to light, Mr. Brodhead as the first scientific historian of this period should receive due acknowledgment for his pioneer labors—of priceless worth since the destruction by fire of the State Archives in the Capitol at Albany.

With the steady growth in the past twenty years of general interest in matters of history and biography, further research among early records of state in Holland, England, and the American Colonies has brought within reach of the general public a number of documents relating to the very earliest settlements in the New Netherland. By these later investigations it now appears clearly established that, while the Dutch were first in the field as explorers and traders, the Belgian-French were their predecessors as actual settlers with homes, families, cattle and tilled fields. The first to bring their wives and children, the first to plow and plant, the first to build permanent residences upon the island of Manhattan and the site of New York City, were a company of Walloons recruited and enrolled by Jesse De Forest of Avesnes—not included as a negligible minority in a colony planned by the Dutch Government, but gathered together of their own motion and wish, as a racial and religious unit, seeking from the United Netherlands only permission to make a settlement, and means of transportation. It is of this Walloon colony, of its leader, Jesse De Forest, and of the part it played in the first days of New Amsterdam, that the present paper in a modest way seeks to treat.

Walloon Founding of New Amsterdam

II. Walloons in General

A. Racial History and Distribution.—The word "*Walloon*" is probably akin to the Anglo-Saxon "wealas," Welsh, Foreigners; and to the German "welsche," strangers. It is commonly applied to the mediæval and modern descendants of Celtic or Alpine stock who have tenaciously held for centuries to the soil where Cæsar found them. He describes them as the eastern division of the Gaulish tribes, the "fortissimi Belgae," dwelling nearest to the Germans "with whom they continually wage war." Not Cimbrian nor Teuton, not Roman nor Frankish, not purely Celtic; probably Celtic with an admixture of Germanic, and perhaps of Frankish blood, the Walloons have never been dislodged from their ancestral ground where, so far as modern knowledge goes, they were well-rooted two thousand years ago. They belong to "the cock-pit of Europe"—about three million in the Belgian provinces of Liège, Namur, Brabant, Hainault and Luxembourg; about one million in the French departments of Aisne, Ardennes, Calais and Nord. Since modern Belgium did not become a separate kingdom until 1830, the terms Belgic or Belgian-French, as applied to this Walloon element, are not political, but racial or geographical. In terms of present national borders, we may say that, roughly, the Walloon territory, at the period of which we are chiefly speaking, was that now included in southwest Belgium and northeast France. It is hardly necessary to point out to what an extent this territory has been trampled under both political and religious conflicts. Kings and powerful nobles schemed, wrangled, lied, married and murdered for possession of the soil. Bought or conquered, the rich provinces were harried and plundered, drained of blood and treasure. Boundaries ceaselessly shifted between France and the Spanish Netherlands, even before political and military wars were empoisoned with acute religious differences.

B. CHARACTERISTICS. — Race characteristics appear strongly defined and persistent. They are a stocky, rather short, type, of rugged health, dark skin, and most often black hair. They are not of a stolid temperament, but quick to love, fight, pray or laugh. They appear to have been always a fighting and a home-loving people—patriotic and warlike (at all events, sturdy soldiers), deeply religious, and tenacious of their liberties. They formerly spoke Liégeois (a middle French dialect) in which a considerable literature remains, of marked peculiarities and some merit. In later centuries they have spoken ordinary, somewhat provincial, modern French.

C. RELIGION.—With the spread of the Reformation and the rise of the Protestant Netherlands, Spanish persecution became most bitter. Though the southern provinces contained more adherents to the elder faith than the northern ones, yet the former contained many thousands of Huguenots who finally had to choose between extermination and expatriation. Hainault,[1] although farther from Spain, fared no better than the south.

[1] Ceded by the French to Spain in 1559.

Walloon Founding of New Amsterdam

D. EMIGRATION DUE TO PERSECUTION.—From all these Inquisition-ridden, tortured provinces Huguenots, and especially Walloons, poured north and east to escape the talons of Spain. Many reached England, some others penetrated into Prussia; the majority found an asylum in Holland. There was no question of gathering together their forces for a possible return. Their beautiful and beloved country, home of their stock for more than twenty centuries, lay open to the power of the tyrant. It is naturally indefensible. There are no "coigns of vantage" from which to repel an intruder. Allegiance to the Belgian soil has ever been a liability rather than an asset—so far at least as earthly safety goes.

The refugees, while doubtless in many cases migrating at severe financial loss, were far from being social derelicts. They paid their scot wherever they went. Thankful for Holland's religious toleration, naturally law-abiding, both industrious and ingenious, the Walloons were made welcome everywhere.

"Carrying with them a knowledge of the arts, in which they were great proficients," says Brodhead,[1] "they were distinguished in their new home for their tasteful and persevering industry. To the Walloons the Dutch were probably indebted for much of the repute which they gained as a nation in many branches of manufactures."

J. W. De Forest,[2] also, quotes "another modern investigator, the Netherlands historian Archer," as

[1] "History of the State of New York," by John R. Brodhead, N. Y. 1853, Ch. V, p. 147.
[2] "The De Forests of Avesnes and of New Netherland," J. W. De Forest, 1900.

5

declaring that "the whole greatness of Holland sprang from her hospitality to a hundred thousand exiled Walloon families."

These Belgian-French Protestant refugees, not speaking Dutch, naturally wished to establish their own church services. The tolerant Hollanders saw no objection to this. Religious freedom was the essence of the hospitality sought and granted. The Walloon Church was then soon established, with the use of the French language and the Geneva Catechism, and to this day the strangers' descendants in Holland so worship.

By the time the war between France and Spain closed with the treaty of 1598, the worst—Alva's unspeakable worst—was nearly over for the Netherlands. The half century preceding had been one of horror, too well known to need repetition. The seven northern provinces of the Netherlands[1] had declared their independence by the Union of Utrecht in 1579, after the heroic and famous defense of Leyden; and, while their great leader, William the Silent, had been assassinated in 1584, the Dutch dauntlessly fought on to formal recognition of independence from Spain in 1609. The ten southern provinces, on the other hand, were crushed; Protestantism had been practically wiped out. Thoroughly cowed, they returned to Spanish allegiance, not to raise a national head again until the second quarter of the nineteenth century; and to the present time Catholicism is the prevailing faith.

[1] Protestant Dutch.

Walloon Founding of New Amsterdam

The latter half of the sixteenth century had been one of frightful misery for both northern and southern provinces. During this time it is estimated that at least half a million Walloons had emigrated, for the most part to Holland. Perhaps an additional hundred thousand had been slain. Civilization was at a standstill.

Strange to say, while the little Dutch republic had been so struggling and suffering, with dikes cut, fields ruined, towns leveled, she had been steadily growing in wealth by commerce and manufactures.[1] After the defeat of the Armada[2] Spain could no longer check her sea power; the young nation of the United Netherlands speedily became mistress of the seas. National pride, stimulated by victory, made all things possible. Hence the Walloon immigrants, although entering at a time of storm and stress, were made welcome, kept busy and well paid, and speedily made to share in the rising prosperity of the whole country. To their leaders, indeed, the chief doubt was lest they should become lost by assimilation into the larger element of the Dutch about them.

III. COMPARISON OF THE WALLOON COLONY IN LEYDEN WITH THE CONTEMPORARY PURITAN COLONY FROM ENGLAND IN LEYDEN.

A. PREVIOUS EXPERIENCE OF EACH COLONY.—Most persons, perhaps, are wont to think of the

[1] "Modern History," by W. M. West, passim.
[2] 1588.

The De Forests and the

religious persecutions of this age as wholly like to that to which the Walloons were subjected; namely, the persecution of Protestants by Catholics. They do not realize that in England at the same time, for example, there was a persecution of "Dissenters," by the Established Church, scarcely less cruel or unjust. Queen Elizabeth seems to have enjoyed an undeserved reputation for being comparatively tolerant. It is true that she used in office talented men regardless of their creeds; and she discouraged public discussions of religion; but she set her hand to laws and acts of extreme intolerance. She herself said[1] that while "she would suppress the papistical religion so that it should not grow, she would root out Puritanism and the favorers thereof." The persecution of the Anabaptist refugees from the continent in 1575, resulting in the dispersion of the whole group, with the burning alive of several at Smithfield, indicates her general attitude. "In 1581," says Campbell,[2] "some acts were passed by Parliament which, aimed primarily at the Catholics, bore heavily upon the nonconformists." In 1583, the High Commission Court was established for the express purpose of harrying the latter, especially the clergy, who were much better educated than those of the Established Church. Through this instrument, and by the zealous labors of Whitgift, Archbishop of Canterbury, and Aylmer, Bishop of London, hounding of the Puritan leaders increased.

[1]"The Puritans of Holland, England, and America," by Douglass Campbell, p. 490.
[2]"The Puritans of Holland, England and America," by Douglass Campbell, p. 492.

Walloon Founding of New Amsterdam

"In nothing did this Commission [1] fall behind Alva's famous Council of Blood, created fifteen years before, except in the power of punishing by death; and in the condition of the English prisons of that day, even this power was indirectly granted, for the jail-fever was as fatal as the axe of the executioner. Of its origin, the unimpassioned Hallam [2] says, "The primary model was the Inquisition itself."

It should be understood, of course, that the Puritans labored long and patiently in England to remedy the shocking immorality and illiteracy which existed, protected by the Crown, within the Church of England; that for the most part they became Separatists only when flung out neck and crop, and "Pilgrims" only when driven into exile to preserve a bare minimum of intelligent opinion or personal freedom. Under such circumstances, at Scrooby in Lincolnshire, in the first decade of the seventeenth century, was gathered the famous group of Separatists who shortly, like the Walloons, were driven to seek the peace of religious toleration under the friendly flag of the Netherlands; and like them, also, to venture among the very first who braved the unknown terrors of the New World.

The Separatists, having endured the severest persecutions, finally determined to emigrate—the first, from London, as early as 1593. From Scrooby, in 1606, two more bands of refugees departed, and in 1608, the remainder, after being betrayed, plundered,

[1] Campbell, p. 494.
[2] "Constitutional History," by J. H. Hallam, Vol. 1, p. 204.

The De Forests and the

imprisoned and scattered in the effort to escape,[1] finally reached Holland. They were under the leadership of their pastor, the Rev. John Robinson, a man of great learning, courage, and breadth of mind, a Cambridge man and an ordained clergyman of the Church of England who remained not only the head of the Puritan Church of the Netherlands, but also— what is perhaps not so generally known—the only pastor of the Pilgrim colony at Plymouth from their landing in 1620 until his death in 1625. A touching account of the terrors and cruelties of the persecution preceding and accompanying the flight is given in quaint old language by Governor Bradford in his History "Of Plimoth Plantation," of which the original MS. was a few years ago returned to the Commonwealth of Massachusetts by the British Government. He comments also,

"Mr. Foxe recordeth how y^t besids those worthy martirs & confessors which were burned in queen Marys days & otherwise tormented, many (both students & others) fled out of ye land, to ye number of 800. And became severall congregations. At Wesell,[2] Frankford, Bassill, Emden, Markpurge, Strausborugh & Geneva &c."[3]

Bradford continues regarding the exiles from Scrooby[4] . . . "They could not long continue in any peaceable condition, but were hunted & persecuted on every side, so as their former afflictions

---

[1] "Of Plimoth Plantation," by Gov. William Bradford, pp. 2-25.
[2] Peter Minuit the Walloon, third Governor of New Amsterdam, was a deacon in this refugee church at Wesel.
[3] "Of Plimoth Plantation," p. 6.
[4] Bradford, p. 15.

Walloon Founding of New Amsterdam

were but as flea-bitings in comparison with those that now came upon them. . . . Seeing them selves thus molested, and that ther was no hope of their continuance ther, by a joynte consente they resolved to goe into ye Low Countries, wher they hearde was freedome of Religion for all men."

The experiences of this colony under Robinson form in many respects a close parallel with those of the Walloon refugees of whom De Forest became the leader. Driven by the crass ignorance and bitter piety of those in authority, Robinson's Protestant colony came to Amsterdam in 1608, removed to Leyden in 1609, and emigrated to America in 1620. Jesse De Forest's father emigrated to Leyden in 1602, Jesse himself in 1615, many of their relatives and friends in the intervening years. In 1623 De Forest's colony of Walloons followed the example of the English Protestants in adventuring to find a permanent home upon the western continent.

B. FELLOWSHIP IN LEYDEN.—The two colonies must have had much in common. Alike in religion and general characteristics, with experiences in many ways very similar, strangers in a strange land, together at the same time for conscience' sake, finding much the same problems and opportunities, they were doubtless well informed of each other's fortunes. Bradford says, "ye magistrate of y^t citie"[1] compared the English refugees with "the Walloons who were of ye French church in y^t citie," somewhat to the disparagement of the latter as being more prone to quarrel among themselves than the less mercurial

[1] Leyden. Bradford, p. 27.

The De Forests and the

British. Says Mrs. Robert De Forest,[1] "It is known that much cordiality and friendship existed between these French and English Protestants." This is the more likely when we remember that many thousands of Walloons in the latter half of the sixteenth century passed into England as well as into Holland. According to Froude,[2] the Spanish ambassador, in 1562, reported over 30,000 Flemish refugees in England. In 1587 there were in Norwich alone nearly 5,000 Walloons, making a majority of the population,[3] "So late as 1645,[4] when Laud had driven great numbers away, there were 700 communicants in the Dutch church at Colchester, 500 in Sandwich, and 900 in the Walloon church at Canterbury."

The material prosperity of modern England, of Holland, and of colonial America was unquestionably increased by this migration of Walloon refugees, every one of whom was a skilled artisan. In this they had the advantage over the Pilgrims, who, as Bradford laments,[5] "were not acquainted with trade nor traffique (by which y^t countrie doth subsiste) but had only been used to a plaine countrie life & ye inocente trade of husbandrey." One reason why the English roused to reemigration before the Walloons, and in greater numbers, from that "faire and bewtifull citie" of Leyden, was that the former, being

[1] "A Walloon Family in America," p. 17.
[2] "History of England," by J. A. Froude, Vol. VII, pp.270, 413.
[3] Campbell, p. 489.
[4] Idem, p. 490.
[5] "Of Plimoth Plantation," p. 16.

Walloon Founding of New Amsterdam

unaccustomed to the artisan life of a city, found the confinement detrimental to the health of their young people, as well as social temptations a menace to morals. Recent search, having uncovered so many new sources of value, may still bring to light documents showing a closer interchange of ideas between these two bodies of refugees, or between their leaders, than we are at present justified in assuming. The difference in language was doubtless some bar. De Forest, while not a highly educated man, wrote French well and readily. The important papers concerning his expedition are in his own handwriting, and for the most part bear his signature alone. Robinson was of course a man of signal culture, especially in a day when even high officials and ecclesiastics were so illiterate and so densely ignorant. He was M. A. and Fellow of Cambridge University, a ready scholar in Latin, Greek and Hebrew, a man of native ability and liberal learning, considered, even in those days of bitter prejudice, a distinct loss to the English Church. His opponents admitted him to be [1] "the most learned, polished, and modest spirit that ever separated from the Church of England." Presumably he spoke French, and doubtless both he and De Forest, through long residence in Leyden, spoke Dutch as well as their mother tongue. The Puritan colony centered about Robinson's residence (their place of worship) on the Klockstrasse, opposite St. Peter's Church. If De Forest's group

[1] Appleton's Cyclopedia of American Biography.

The De Forests and the

of colonists had such a center, and whether, if so, it was near that of the Pilgrims, I am unable to say.

C. EMIGRATION OF PART OF THE SEPARATIST CHURCH UNDER ROBINSON IN LEYDEN TO AMERICA IN 1620.—
The fourth chapter of Bradford,[1] "Showing ye reasons & causes of their remoovall," gives a discussion of political, business and social conditions in Leyden, with the arguments for and against emigration, of which almost every sentence applies with equal force to Puritans and to Walloons. It furnishes the basis for a fine understanding of the spirit in which both Robinson and De Forest pursued their courageous designs of leading colonies of their compatriots far across the seas into an unknown wilderness.

(To fearful ones)—"It was answered, that all great and honourable actions are accompanied with great difficulties, and must be both enterprised and overcome with answerable courages. It was granted ye dangers were great, but not desperate; the difficulties were many, but not invincible. For though their were many of them likly, yet they were not certaine; it might be sundrie of ye things feared might never befale; others by provident care & ye use of good means, might in a great measure be prevented; and all of them, through ye help of God, might either be borne, or overcome. True it was, that such attempts were not to be made and undertaken without good ground & reason; not rashly or lightly as many have done for curiositie or hope of gaine, &c. But their condition was not ordinarie; their ends were good &

[1] "History of Plimoth Plantation," pp. 29-35.

Walloon Founding of New Amsterdam

honourable; their calling lawfulle, & urgente; and therefore they might expecte ye blessing of God in their proceeding. Yea, though they should loose their lives in this action, yet might they have comforte in the same, and their endeavors would be honourable. They lived hear but as men in exile, & in a poor condition; and as greate miseries might possibly befale them in this place, for ye 12 years of truce were now out, & there was nothing but beating of drumes, and preparing for warr, the events whereof are allway uncertaine. Ye Spaniard might prove as cruell as the salvages of America, and ye famine and pestelence as sore hear as ther, & their libertie less to looke out for remedie. After many other perticuler things answered & aledged on both sids, it was fully concluded by ye major parte, to put this designe in execution, and to prosecute it by the best means they could."

D. STIMULUS TO EMIGRATION OF THE WALLOONS.—In view of De Forest's Guiana project, and his efforts to emigrate to Virginia, it is of interest to note that the Pilgrims had much the same experiences.

"Some," says Bradford,[1] "had thoughts & were ernest for Guiana, or some of those fertill places in those hott climats; others were for some parts of Virginia."

The negotiations in regard to both expeditions—that of the English to Plymouth, and that of the

[1] Bradford, p. 34.

The De Forests and the
Walloons to Manhattan—were carried on at almost the same time, the English preceding step for step by about three years, and were in many respects much alike; for example, both colonies tried first to make the settlement in Guiana, then did their best to arrange one in Virginia, and finally decided upon a more northern destination. It is possible that the two bands had even had some idea of making common cause in the New World. The Pilgrim colony on the "Mayflower," as we know, was bound for the mouth of the Hudson, but encountering many delays and adventures en route, so that they reached the American coast only when winter was well upon them, they were halted upon the nearer, more northern shore of Massachusetts by inclement weather and the lateness of the season. Accounts of the Pilgrim voyage and settlement, however, are legion. The parallel with the Walloon expedition will become apparent in subsequent pages.

"The Pilgrim Fathers had gone to America under a patent from the Virginia Company," remarks Mrs. Robert De Forest,[1] "and some of Jesse De Forest's compatriots had gone with them. It was, therefore, quite natural, all things considered, that Jesse himself should propose to emigrate with his followers under the same auspices."

At all events, by the time the remnant of the Mayflower colony had weathered the first winter, he had gathered together between fifty and sixty families, containing about three hundred persons, of

[1] "A Walloon Family in America," by Mrs. Robert W. de Forest, p. 18.

Walloon Founding of New Amsterdam

Protestant Belgian-French who were desirous of making the venture. Before proceeding, however, some account is in order of this one conspicuous leader of the Walloons, Jesse De Forest.

IV. JESSE DE FOREST, LEADER OF THE WALLOON MIGRATION TO NEW NETHERLAND

A. FRENCH ORIGIN AND EARLY CONNECTIONS.— The province of Hainault has long been a land of history and romance. Here dwelt and fought the Nervii, who so earned the respect of Cæsar for their fighting qualities. Baldwin, the Emperor of Byzantium, "Philippa of Hainault," the Queen who sucked the poison from her husband's wound, Froissart, the quaint chronicler, Count Egmont of undying fame— the little plot of ground has furnished its share of notables. Near the Belgian-French frontier, not far from Mons of recent bloodshed and a new legend, stands—or stood, perhaps, until the swift destruction of the past by the present—a little old walled town of fewer than five thousand inhabitants—Avesnes. It has changed hands many times, belonging now to Bavaria, now to Burgundy; a possession in turn of Spain, Austria, France of today. In 1477, Louis XI of France, planning to surprise the Netherlands of Burgundy, sent an army which, on its way, by treachery slew nearly all the people of the town, and after pillage so burned it that but eight dwellings, with a hospital and a monastery, remained. All previous church and town records were destroyed at this

The De Forests and the

time. Somehow the town rose again, for nearly a century later[1] it appears worth being formally ceded from France to Spain. During the French Revolution, some of the town records were used for wadding cartridges, and a hundred years ago, during the invasion of the Prussians, the explosion of a magazine all but destroyed the town once more. Hence the records are very fragmentary.

The earliest known are in the Bibliothèque Nationale at Paris. Others are to be found in the archives of Lille, Mons, etc. These Paris archives run back to 1488; those of Avesnes, broken as they are, begin in 1529. Hundreds[2] of local records, more or less clearly connected, contain the name of De Forest, indicating that the family had been long on the soil. Presently emerge, with fair probability of identification, entries such as any self-respecting old-world community makes every effort to keep, of births and deaths, baptisms and marriages, for the two or three generations immediately preceding Jesse De Forest, the Walloon emigrant.

For the past three centuries, while America in general is very lax in such matters, the records of this particular family, now quite numerous, have been fairly well preserved. Actuated frankly by a mixture of general historic interest and family pride, several De Forests of the present day have been at considerable pains to search the old records available in America, France, Belgium, Holland and England for any entries concerning their immigrant ancestors.

[1] 1559.
[2] "The De Forests of Avesnes," by J. W. De Forest, 1900. (Passim)

Walloon Founding of New Amsterdam

In this they have been fairly successful. While in their published results many pages are naturally devoted to mere genealogical matter affecting later generations, the appendices contain certified copies of records from European archives and similar source-material—of primary interest to the family, no doubt, but also of a certain impersonal value as aiding the general reader to gain a more accurate knowledge of the circumstances under which such important cities as Albany and New York were founded. The two books including this source-material are "The De Forests of Avesnes and of New Netherland," by J. W. De Forest (1900) and "A Walloon Family in America," by Mrs. Robert W. De Forest (1914). While they are informal in style, occasionally gossipy, careful references are given for all statements of any weight, due notice is given whenever evidence passes into speculation, and in general the volumes are free from raw heraldic claims or the like undemocratic pretensions.

According to these old local records, Jean de Forest, father of Jesse de Forest, married Anne Maillard in Avesnes, about 1570, some two years after William of Orange's first defeat by Alva. He belonged to the guild of the wool merchants, as did also several of his brothers.[1] Jean, the youngest of the family, and less often mentioned in the records, very probably was going to and fro as agent for the De Forest wool firm. Markets must have been very uncertain in this half-century of fierce strife between

---
[1] Two others were canons of the church of St. Nicholas in Avesnes.

The De Forests and the

Spain and Protestantism. Jean de Forest, the first Protestant of the family, soon found it necessary to leave his home. In 1601 he appears established as a merchant in Sedan.[1] His family was then scattered: a son, Melchior, at Lille; another, Gerard, at Leyden; a daughter, Anne, with her mother at Amsterdam; only Jesse remaining with his father. Jesse's marriage presently appears.[2]

"1601. Sunday, 23d day of said month[3] at the Catechism, the said Sieur du Tilloy blessed the marriage of Jesse des forests, son of Jean des forests merchant residing in this city, with marie du Cloux, daughter of Nicaise du Cloux merchant residing in this city."

In due time, at intervals on the same register occur entries of the baptisms of the first five children, including Henry or Hendrick,[4] who was later one of the early settlers of New Amsterdam.

B. FAMILY MIGRATION TO HOLLAND.—During these years the family became re-united in Holland. In local records[5] we find, "Received member of the church at Leyden by letter from Beighem op Zoom, Jehan de Forest and Anne Maillard, his wife." Next year[6] they are received members at Amsterdam by letters from Leyden.

"1615, March 1, Baptized at Leyden, Jesse, son of Jesse du Forest and of Marie du Clou."

[1] Holland Records. Registers of the Walloon churches. 1601.
[2] Register of the Huguenot Church in Sedan.
[3] September.
[4] March 7, 1606.
[5] Holland Records. Register of the Walloon Church at Leyden. 1603.
[6] 1604.

Walloon Founding of New Amsterdam

"1616, July 10, Baptized at Leyden, Isaac, son of Jesse du Forest."[1]

C. REASONS LEADING TO EMIGRATION.—Many other entries are at hand, of birth, marriage, church membership, concerning Isaac De Forest, his parents and brothers. Land transactions, voyages, wills, guardianships, and so on are also recorded in numbers, sometimes in French, sometimes in Dutch. Had De Forest been altogether prosperous, he would presumably have remained in one place or in one occupation. On the contrary, the records between 1600 and 1625 show him with an increasingly large family, shifting from place to place, now apparently traveling buyer or salesman for the family firm, again appearing less as a wool merchant than as a dyer. In 1608 he is noted[2] as a "merchant-dyer" upon the records of Montcornet in Thierache.[3] After this we lose sight of him for some years, during which he may have had several children, since the births of five are previously recorded at Sedan, and five more, after this gap in the family records, at Leyden. Later, also, is recorded the marriage of a daughter not included in either group. In 1618 we come across a civic record at The Hague, which tells of his pledging his very dyery-chaldron[4] because he is in arrears of house-rent to the amount of fifty florins. These circumstances indicate that the family was not

[1] Holland Records. Register of the Walloon Church at Leyden.
[2] "De Forests of Avesnes," p. 53.
[3] An eastern canton of Picardy.
[4] "De Forests of Avesnes," p. 56.

prosperous, and may have furnished sufficient spur to emigration.

Still, we must remember that poverty was no slur upon character in those days, especially among Huguenot and Walloon exiles. The very word "Beggar" indeed, flung at them as a scornful epithet, was worn as a proud title. In 1566 some 500 Protestant nobles of the Netherlands (later joined by many of lesser rank) having pledged themselves to make a stand against Spanish cruelty and tyranny, presented a petition to the Duchess of Parma. One of her advisers spoke contemptuously of "les Gueux" (the beggars). The acknowledgment, "Faithful to religion and native land, even to the bearing of the beggar's wallet," soon became a slogan which changed the insult to a distinction. The phrase and the fact behind it became an inheritance of pride in the Protestant Netherlands. Hardship often but breeds dauntlessness; and it may be noted that great adventurers have most often been men with broken fortunes to mend.

V. Efforts of De Forest to Arrange for the Emigration of a Colony Under Auspices of the British Virginia Company

A. Interview with Sir Dudley Carleton, British Ambassador to the Netherlands.—While the formation of the Dutch West India Company had been under discussion for a year, it was not yet organized; hence in July, 1621, De Forest

Walloon Founding of New Amsterdam

went to The Hague,[1] and presenting himself at the residence of the British Ambassador, Sir Dudley Carleton, formally made request, as spokesman for three hundred others, that an expedition, bearing a permanent colony to the New World, might be arranged for them.

B. WRITTEN TRANSACTIONS.—Upon Carleton's suggestion that he present his request in written form, De Forest reappeared two days later with these "Demands," clearly and properly couched, over his own signature, and also a document known as "the round robin." These two papers, brought to Carleton upon July 21, were forwarded by him the same day to Sir George Calvert, then State Secretary. With them went a letter, saying,

"There hath been with me of late a certain Walon in the name of divers families, men of all trades and occupations, who desire to goe into Virginia. . . . I required of him his demands in writing, with the signatures of such as were to bear part therein, both of which I send your honour herewith."

As the documents presented by De Forest both bear date of July 21, while Carleton's letter is headed July 19, it would appear that unless either had been slightly misdated, Carleton's letter, in spite of the wording, had been held two days, after being written on the day of his interview with De Forest, until the required papers were made ready to accompany it. The discrepancy, however, is a trifling one, and does not affect the substance of the contents.

[1] Brodhead, Ch. V., pp. 146, 147.

The De Forests and the

The petition known as "The Demands"[1] requested from the British Virginia Company definite replies upon seven points of inquiry, as follows:[2]

1. Defense by the King, and freedom of religion;
2. Transportation of the colonists in an armed vessel, and later freightage of supplies;
3. Choice of location after landing;
4. Permission to fortify the settlement, and to set up local self-government;
5. Furnishing of ammunition and permission to make powder, shot and cannon;
6. Sole right to the territory within a radius of eight miles, "and whether those of them who could live as nobles would be permitted to style themselves such";
7. Game, fishery, mineral and timber rights.

After incidental request for information regarding the warehouse ordinances of London, with a view to establishing trade relations, the document closes with proffer of full allegiance, and the usual formal courtesies.

Accompanying this was a "round-robin" agreement[3] of the colonists prepared to go upon the proposed expedition. It is 18 x 13.5 inches in size. Within the small inner oval are a few words[4] promising that the signers would settle in Virginia "under

---

[1] N. Y. Colonial Documents, Vol. III.
London Documents I, p. 9, for rather loose translation.
Baird, Vol. I, pp. 348-350 for full document in French.
J. W. De Forest for better translation. "A Walloon Family," Vol. II, p. 17, for facsimile.   [2] Condensed.
[3] Facsimile, Baird, I, p. 351: also "A Walloon Family," Vol. II, p. 21.
[4] The language, of course, is French.

Walloon Founding of New Amsterdam

the conditions set forth in the articles which we have communicated." Time and the fold have blurred the central part, but the close stands out coolly enough: "And not otherwise." In the next oval come the clear signatures [1] of the men—"Jesse de Forest, tincturieur"; "Mousnier de la Montagne, estudient en medicine," etc.; while in the outer oval, opposite each man's name, appears his family condition—"homme a marier," perhaps, or "fme dix enfans," as the case might be.

These two papers, presented to Carleton within forty-eight hours, apparently show De Forest to have been both business-like, and eager to be gone. In a fortnight or so came the categorical reply from the Virginia Company[2] through the "Rt. Ho'ble Sr George Calvert," in substance as follows:

1. "If it stand with his Ma'ties gratious favour, they do not conceive it any inconvenience at present to suffer sixtie families of Walloones and ffrenchmen not exceeding the number of 300 persons to goe and inhabite in Virginia. . . . the said persons taking oath to . . . bee conformable to . . . the Churche of England.

2. They esteeme it so Royall a favour in his Ma'tie and so singular a benefitt to the said Walloons and ffrenchmen to bee admitted to live in that fruitfull land under . . . so mightie and pious a Monarch as his Ma'tie is that they ought not to expect of his sacred Ma'tie any ayde of shipping or

---
[1] Of fifty-six, only three made their marks.
[2] N. Y. Col. Doc. Vol. III. London Doc. I.

other chargeable favour . . . only in point of advise and Councell."

"3, 4, 5, 6, 7. ARTICLES. They conceive that for the prosperity and principally the securing of the plantacion in His Ma'ties obedience it is not expedient that the sayd ffamilies should bee sett downe in one gross bodie" . . . but, in short, be thoroughly broken up and scattered among "the naturall Englishe; and this course they out of their experience do conceive likely to prove better and more comfortable to the sayd Walloons and ffrenchmen than that other w'ch they desire."

C. RESULT ON PLANS OF THE WALLOONS.— Whether "Jesse de Forest, tincturieur," mingled any other emotion with the disappointment in which he must have received "so Royall a favour" is not recorded. He made no further effort to gain the ear of "so mightie and pious a Monarch," but for eight months quietly perfected other plans.

VI. EFFORTS OF DE FOREST TO ARRANGE FOR THE EMIGRATION OF A COLONY UNDER DUTCH AUSPICES

A. PETITION TO THE STATES OF HOLLAND AND WEST FRIESLAND.—Seeing that the organization of the West India Company was proceeding with true Dutch deliberation, the undaunted De Forest in April, 1622, took his petition to the provincial legislature called "The States of Holland and West Friesland," using in his request the term "West

Walloon Founding of New Amsterdam

Indies," which then included the whole eastern coast of North and South America. On being consulted, the Directors of the Dutch West India Company[1] reported briefly in favor of promoting the plan. As no action followed, De Forest four months later renewed his efforts, turning now to the States General.[2] The matter was referred back to the States of Holland and West Friesland,[3] which formally authorized[4] "the said Jesse des Forest" to "inscribe and enroll for the colonies all families having the qualifications requisite," and "to furnish a report thereof to the Lords Gentlemen." The outcome of this was "The Guiana Expedition."

VII. DE FOREST'S EXPEDITION TO GUIANA UNDER DUTCH WEST INDIA COMPANY

A. GENERAL STAGE OF COLONIZATION IN SOUTH AMERICA.—In the early part of the seventeenth century, Holland, being freed from Spanish oppression, had rapidly risen to sea-power and to schemes of wide colonial expansion. Admiral Willekens, with one great fleet, was to take Brazil from Spain by sudden attack. Another commander, with an equally large squadron of war-ships, was to support Willekens by keeping the Atlantic swept clean of the Spanish. A third fleet was to take possession of the Congo and Angola coasts, in order to supply gold and slaves. Atlantic settlements north of the Poto-

[1] Royal Archives, The Hague, Holland.
[2] The national legislative body of the United Netherlands.
[3] N. Y. Col. Doc. British Doc. from State Archives at The Hague.
[4] Aug. 27, 1622.

The De Forests and the

mac were more or less under consideration, since Dutch explorers had now for some years led the way. The organization of the Dutch West India Company, as its name implies, was leading to large plans for trade and colonization in that quarter of the globe, notably among the Caribbean Islands and along the northern coast of South America between the Gulf of Maracaibo and the frontier of Brazil. The latter region was called interchangeably "Guiana" and "The Wild Coast" by writers of this time. All of these projects were upon a scale to command respect. Willekens' expedition,[1] for example, was carried by twenty-three ships and three clipper yachts, defended in transit by five hundred cannon; and consisted of sixteen hundred sailors, and seventeen hundred soldiers, besides civilian colonists. It has been thought by some that De Forest's band were of these last, but later-found sources show clearly that he left in the previous June.

B. SAILING ROUTES TO THE NEW WORLD.—Before going further, it may be well to recall two facts, perfectly well known, but liable to be overlooked since the same conditions no longer prevail. The first is that the present lanes of travel on the North Atlantic were then unknown. Vessels from Holland, bound for the mouth of the Hudson, slipped down the west coast of Africa, past the mouth of the Congo, across the narrowest part of the Atlantic to perhaps the mouth of the Wyapoko on the frontier between Brazil and Guiana; then northward among

[1] Wassenaer, passim.

Walloon Founding of New Amsterdam

the West Indies and on up the coast of the present United States. For the return voyage, explains Wassenaer, "on leaving the lower river,[1] you lay your course for the west wind, and, having got it, to the Bermudas, whence homeward by the current." "The Wild Coast"—say the present Dutch Guiana—for a Hollander was as much on the way to New York as Buffalo, for a Chicago man, is on the way to Boston. Vessels clearing the Hook of Holland, one bound for Manhattan and the other for Maracaibo, were strictly in company.

The other point is that South America has always seemed to Europe of more importance than the easy egotism of "the States" realizes. What is true even today, with the vast wealth and the dense population centering about the island of Manhattan, was a hundred times more true in the beginning of the seventeenth century. The settlement of New York may now seem to us a matter of some importance; it was then a very negligible affair, to both English and Dutch, as may be seen by the delays and difficulties encountered by Jesse de Forest in his ceaseless endeavors to get permission and transportation for hundreds of desirable colonists already recruited and enrolled. Holland paid scant heed to the proposition of making a settlement upon the River of the Moon, whence, at most, she expected to draw a few furs and a little tobacco. It was not a North Atlantic Company the Dutch were organizing, but one for the West Indies. From South America and the

[1] The mouth of the Hudson.

The De Forests and the

Caribbean Islands, already exploited by Spain, they looked for coffee and spices, dye-woods, gold, jewels, furniture-woods. Less was to be feared here from either climate or natives. Manhattan was the little-known, little-visited end of the "spur track" far beyond the "main-traveled road" leading to the West Indies. At a time when the interest of many influential Hollanders was centered upon "The Wild Coast," and when, as previously noted, many of the Puritan colony in Leyden—"and none of the meanest"—argued strongly in favor of emigrating to Guiana as being a far more promising place for a colony than New Netherland or New England, it need be matter of little surprise when we find Jesse De Forest organizing at the same time two colonies, one for Guiana, the other for New Netherland, launching them ten weeks apart, and himself accompanying to Guiana the first of these.

C. WASSENAER'S "HISTORICAL ACCOUNT." — As authority for a discussion of this Guiana enterprise, two reliable sources have long been available, and a third has very recently been brought to light. The first is the history of "The New World, or Description of the West Indies," by John De Laet, one of the leading directors of the West India Company. Brodhead mentions this [1] as being published in Leyden in 1625, and as having been made up from "various manuscript journals[2] of different captains and pilots," including Hendrik Hudson's private journal, and

[1] Brodhead, Ch. V., p. 157.
[2] Mentioned definitely as used.

Walloon Founding of New Amsterdam

also, apparently, the original reports of Block, Mey and Christiansen. Brodhead notes that "from this circumstance its historical authority is nearly equal to that of an original record," and continues [1]: "Until the recent reference to the earlier 'Historical Relation' of Wassenaer, which contains a general statement of interesting events in Europe and America from 1621 to 1632,[2] the work of De Laet was thought to contain the first published account of the Dutch province. Its authority is deservedly very high— and had English and American writers consulted its accurate pages, less injustice would perhaps have been done to the Hollanders. . . ."—and, incidentally, to the little band of Walloons who as colonists preceded the Dutch.

Another of these sources is the "Historisches Verhael" of Wassenaer, mentioned above. Brodhead was the first to find[3] a complete copy, and to use it as a historical authority. A good part of it, in translation, is to be found in early volumes of the New York Historical Documents[4] and in the Proceedings of the New York Historical Society.[5]

D. THE JOURNAL OF JESSE DE FOREST.—A third source, and in this connection an even more important one, is a very unusual manuscript journal which has been lying unnoted in the British Museum for many years, being published for the first time[6] in

[1] P. 157.
[2] Wassenaer's own sub-title.
[3] In London.
[4] Vol. III, p. 397.
[5] Year 1848, p. 215.
[6] Either in the original French or in translation.

The De Forests and the

1914. It is listed as Sloane MS. 179 b, having been among the first of similar MSS. collected by Sir Hans Sloane, founder of the Museum. Its full title[1] is, "Journal du voyage faict par les pères de familles envoyes par Mes les Directeurs de la Compagnee des Indes Occidentales pour visiter la coste de Gujane." It is commonly called "Jesse De Forest's Journal," though certainly part of it, and possibly all, is written by another hand than his. It contains a complete account of the expedition of which De Forest was "our Captain," to its finish. The narrative is in itself readably interesting, with ten beautifully colored maps, as many careful descriptions of places, and numerous sketches—of the high-built native houses along the river lowlands, for example.

During the dispute over the boundary line between British Guiana and Venezuela,[2] the British Government published extracts from this MS. to prove that a Dutch colony had been established on the Essequibo River in British Guiana before 1624. This argument was based upon this settlement of the pères de familles[3] headed by De Forest. It was also noted by the Rev. George Edmundson, who discovered it in the course of gathering data for articles on Guiana;[4] and finally published in full in "A Walloon Family."

[1] Both original and translation are given in Mrs. Robert W. De Forest's "A Walloon Family in America," Vol. II, pp. 188-278 (1914).
[2] Settled in 1899.
[3] So quoted by the Government.
[4] Articles on Guiana, English Historical Review, Oct., 1901; Oct., 1903; Jan., 1904.

Walloon Founding of New Amsterdam

E. "LES PÈRES DE FAMILLES."—For two years, as we have seen, Jesse De Forest, with his fixed idea, had been seeking the chance to emigrate. The West India Company was finally organized;[1] and within a fortnight[2] the impatient Walloon, in the ship "Pigeon," left Leyden on his way to the New World. "But as their Excellencies the said Directors thought it better before carrying over the above mentioned families, to send a certaine number of the heads of families with the said Jesse des forests to inspect the region and themselves select their place of abode, there were chosen for this purpose Louis le Maire, Bartheleme Digan, Anthoine Descendre, Anthoine Beaumont, Jehan Godebon, Abraham Douillers, Dominique Masure, the brothers Jehan and Gilles Daynes, and Jehan Mousnier de la Montagne, over whom on landing the said Jesse des forest was to have command."[3]

Four of these men were among those who had signed the Round Robin two years before—"Jesse de Forest, tincturieur"; "Anthoine Descendre, laboureur"; "Barthelemy Digand, scyeur de bois"; and "Jehan Mousnier Montagne, estudient en medecine." The last of these, though still "homme à marier,"[4] we find stoutly enrolled among the "fathers of families." The fact that later, on returning to Leyden, he married De Forest's daughter Rachel, may indicate an already altered footing among the

[1] June 21, 1623.
[2] Saturday, July 1, 1623.
[3] Sloane MS. 179 b, p. 1.
[4] "A man for marriage"—a bachelor.

band. In the Journal, "our Captain always means De Forest"; "Our Master" refers to the commander of the "Pigeon," one Pieter Fredericsz of Harlem.

F. COMPANION VOYAGE OF "THE MACKEREL" AND "THE PIGEON" FROM LEYDEN TO THE NEW WORLD.—Another yacht of about the same size, "The Mackerel," sailed just before "The Pigeon." The ships expected to keep company as far as "the Amazons"; from there "The Mackerel" was to go on to New Netherland. Both vessels planned to coast along under protection of some slave ships headed for the Guinea coast; but slight accidents to "The Mackerel's" mast first lost the opportunity of this protection, and presently made it necessary to anchor in the Downs[1] for further protection.

The "Masters" of both vessels seem to have been in no hurry. Supper parties, fights, a wedding, desertions, and casual piracies occupied two months before even Cape Finisterre was reached. Fredericsz having halted an English ship returning from Newfoundland, and having robbed the sailors' chests of all their clothing, De Forest made him return every stitch; and then, supported by the pilot, demanded that he should leave off "skylarking" by the way, and proceed more directly. At Madeira, in mid September, the little ships parted company, "The Mackerel" then heading for New Netherland. The latter vessel seems also to have spent some time in

[1] Here they had an amusing and stirring adventure with one Pieter Jansz of Flushing, whom Sir Walter Raleigh had met in Cayenne in 1617, and said of him that he "had traded that place about a dussen years." Other of Jansz's tricks appear later in the Journal.

Walloon Founding of New Amsterdam

the popular sport of the high seas. Wassenaer remarks,[1] "The yacht 'Maeckereel' sailed out last year 1623 on the 16th of June and arrived yonder [2] on the 12th of December. That was indeed somewhat late, but it wasted time in the salvage islands to *catch a fish* (a Spanish prize), and did not catch it, so ran the luck."

On October 16th, at the mouth of the Amazon, "The Pigeon" again met Pieter Jansz, and together they sailed in. "The Pigeon" spent about six weeks along the river, exploring and trading. She found it already crowded. Six English and Irish colonies were even then established, though under warning of frequent and imminent trouble from both the Spanish and the natives. On December 4th, "The Pigeon" was back at the North Cape, headed for the Wyapoko River.[3] It was during this leisurely progress that many of the fine maps and sketches in the "Journal" were made. After exploring the Wyapoko for some ten days, the "pères de familles" finally[4] found a place to their liking.

G. THE SETTLEMENT ALONG THE WYAPOKO ON THE WILD COAST.—Here occurred a surprise and disappointment, for the Master of "The Pigeon," Pietersz, then informed them that his orders from the Directors of the West India Company were to leave there all of them except two whom he would

---
[1] Under date of April, 1624.
[2] In New Netherland.
[3] Now called the Oyapok—the present boundary between French Guiana and northern Brazil.
[4] Dec. 27.

allow to return with him. This seemed to them unreasonable—that they had not been allowed to bring their families, nor to know the circumstances before leaving Holland, that they might make arrangements; nor were they now permitted to fetch them. As the Journal says,

"They began in divers ways to excuse themselves. Our Captain, seeing this, declared to the Master that he was ready to remain if they would give him in place of the heads of families who wished to return, the same number of sailors. This was allowed him so that there remained with our said Captain, Louis le Maire and I[1] from among the families, our Gunner, four sailors and the Surgeon's mate—nine persons in all."[2]

The entries next following are very brief:[3]

"On Thursday the 28th they prepared everything which they were willing to give us, which was (illegible) of Coucal,[4] axes, knives, a small pierrier,[5] with our Cheloupe."[6]

"On Friday the 29th we left to go to Commaribo."[7]

"On Saturday the 30th we arrived at the said Commaribo."

"The first day of the year 1624 our ship left to return to Holland."

These "heads of families" seem to have been men

[1] Almost certainly La Montagne.
[2] Journal, 1623, Dec. 27.
[3] No omissions.
[4] Cocoa, presumably.
[5] A cannon for throwing stones; a saker.
[6] "Shallop"; ship's pinnace.
[7] A safer, higher spot across the river.

Walloon Founding of New Amsterdam

of resolution and self-reliance. There is no further expression of surprise, annoyance, or sense of injustice. A letter[1] which was written the last day of December, 1623, to be carried back to Leyden by "The Pigeon," shows excellent courage and spirits. It begins,

"Although the letter from our Captain[2] suffices to inform you both of the success of our voyage and the excellence of this region where we live, I must not neglect to fulfill the promise which I made at our departure. Our voyage was very happily concluded . . . we found very friendly natives here, who treated us well; the streams are convenient and the land overflows with everything that is needed to support human life: good bread and fine fish . . . the bread is superior to the best that is to be found in Holland. . . . Tree fruits have a much finer flavor than in the Netherlands. . . . We expect here the families from Holland[3] . . .;" and continues with various items of intelligent interest.

The Journal continues with frequent entries. De Forest seems to have been an indefatigable explorer and experimenter. Being by trade a dyer, he was constantly on the watch for dyewoods and suitable places for dyeing cotton. He collected mineral specimens, bought tobacco fields, laid off sites for towns and fortifications, made long excursions, and took many notes. He was successful in

[1] Given in full by Wassenaer.
[2] Not given by Wassenaer.
[3] Wassenaer adds, "The families whom they expect are people going thither from Leyden."

The De Forests and the

making friends with the natives and in preserving the peace even between hostile tribes. One incident is given at some length, showing considerable courage, tact, and leadership on the part of "our Captain." A large party of Caribs had come on a visit to the Yaos, the tribe among which De Forest and his little party were living on amicable terms. The next day appeared, in canoes, a third tribe, the Aricoures, in deadly pursuit of the Caribs. The clash was imminent when "as they were preparing to fight, peace was made between them by the intervention of our Captain." The ceremony ingeniously suggested by him is described to the point at which,

"This done, the Caribs, throwing down their arms, rushed into the canoes of the others and embraced them. On the occasion of this peace the Yaos entertained them together for eight days; peace having never been known between them before."

For a man who had been in the region less than three months, without previous knowledge of the native language or customs, this seems to indicate a certain force of character.

Within ten days of De Forest's arrival, he had bought "a field in which to grow tobacco, which cost us four axes"; and in the course of the next three months had laid out fields of sugar and cotton, chosen the sites for their fortified town and their dye-works, and collected the native products needed for this industry. He appears to have recognized on sight the small Oreillan tree from the seeds of which

Walloon Founding of New Amsterdam

the valuable dye called "arnotto" or "bastard scarlet" was made. One of the most valuable products collected for trade was the "letter-wood" or "leopard-wood." This was of a rich dark brown color with odd markings resembling letters, in black. It was hard as ebony and heavier than teak, weighing eighty pounds to the cubic foot; and fetched from 30 to 40 pounds a ton. The colonists from the first speak with vivid interest of going "higher up in the country, along this river, where no Christian has ever been . . . in the hope of finding something curious." One entry of the Journal reads, "On the 27th of September our Captain was at Cayenne to see the Caribs, who receive him kindly."

H. THE DEATH OF DE FOREST.—Eight months had elapsed since the sailing of "The Pigeon," but no returning ship had brought the colonists' families. In the midst of their hopeful activities, misfortune suddenly befell them. On October 13, while on an expedition by canoe, De Forest suffered a severe sunstroke, and was brought home unconscious, with a high fever. The Journal[1] continues,

"On the 15th of October, by the advice of those who had lived in this country before us, we had him bled, which gave him relief; but being impatient of keeping quiet, he wished to go on the sea again, returning from which he again had a sunstroke, which redoubled his fever."

"On the 22nd of October our said Captain died, much regretted by the Christians and Indians, who

[1] La Montagne writing.

had taken a great liking to him. This day we carried him to be buried as honorably as was possible for us, accompanying the body with our arms, which we each discharged three times over his grave, and our cannon as well."

Here then, under an alien sky, in the full vigor of middle life, Jesse De Forest met the sudden death, found the lonely grave, which are the lot of most pioneer adventurers. Like many another, also, the lasting influence of a life so casually cut short upon a distant shore, is to be measured only in the light of later years.

1. THE COLONISTS' RETURN TO HOLLAND.—With De Forest fell the hopes of the colony for which he had so eagerly planned and petitioned and waited. The West India Company apparently made no effort to fulfill its promise of sending out the families. Of the original "pères de familles," only Le Maire and La Montagne remained, with the few sailors left to reenforce them. "Seeing that the ships did not come as they had promised us and that our stores were giving out," the survivors decided that while something still was left, they "ought to try to build some sort of craft with which they could reach the Caribbean Islands." At this, with insufficient tools, they toiled most of the time until the 23rd of May, when they were surprised by the arrival of a boat from the "Flying Dragon," commanded by Gelyn van Stapels of Flushing, who had been with Admiral Lucifer in the valley of "the Amazons." He reported to the little band that he had been commissioned by

Walloon Founding of New Amsterdam

the Directors of the West India Company in the Zeeland Chamber to take them home with him; and nothing loath, they went aboard. The voyage home was a leisurely one, but at length, on Nov. 16, 1625, the survivors "arrived at Flushing, for which God be praised."[1]

VIII. DE FOREST'S CONTEMPORARY WALLOON COLONY FOR THE HUDSON RIVER

A. THE "NIEUWE NEDERLANDT," SKIPPER CORNELIS MEY; DATE OF VOYAGE.—Meanwhile, what of Jesse De Forest's other Walloon colony, destined for the mouth of the Hudson? A number of careful writers[2] have stated on what seemed then good authority that the "Nieuwe Nederlandt" under Cornelis Mey left Holland for the western shores in March of 1623. This would have been before De Forest and La Montagne left for Guiana. Prior to the discovery of "Sloane MS. 179 b," it was thought by some that De Forest went to the New World on the expedition bound for the Hudson instead of that for Guiana. Both these suppositions are now known to be erroneous. Even O'Callaghan, usually reputed careful, though he found the date 1624, altered it as "an error," to correspond with some statements made by Dutch authorities—as, for example, that contained in a memoir[3] drawn up by the West India Company in 1641, which says that "in and since

[1] The closing phrase of the Journal.
[2] See list of authorities in J. W. De Forest, Vol. II, pp. 77-79.
[3] N. Y. Col. Doc. I, p. 564; II, p. 153.

1623 four forts were built in the New Netherlands, to-wit: Amsterdam . . . ." Others have placed undue reliance in the deposition of Caterina Tricot, taken when she was past eighty, when she had forgotten both the name of the ship and that of the captain. Governor Stuyvesant claims the date as 1623. So also does a "Report[1] of the Board of Accounts of New Netherland," dated 1624, which declares, "In the years 1622 and 1623 the West India Company took possession . . . etc."

The weight of recent authority, however, seems wholly in favor of the year 1624 as the date of the earliest settlement. The contemporary Wassenaer, indeed, whose narrative is both careful and consistent, seems to have been overlooked in this discussion. Brodhead, if accepted as authority by later writers—as in most respects he deserves—has doubtless misled the superficial. While familiar with Wassenaer, and indeed quoting him in this very detail, he omits the date given by Wassenaer as not in accordance with the year 1623 on which he—Brodhead—had previously settled. He says[2] "There is a slight discrepancy between Trico's testimony and Wassenaer's account," but does not note or discuss the difference in dates. However, the slow or partial acceptance of an attempt to reform the calendar, about this time, leaves many dates of the early seventeenth century somewhat in doubt, only to be patiently verified. In thousands of records, with a fine impartiality, the date has been recorded

[1] N. Y. Col. Doc. III, pp. 31-32.
[2] Brodhead, pp. 150, 151, and note.

Walloon Founding of New Amsterdam

1623-4, without further comment. Wassenaer, under date of 1624, writes,

"The West India Company . . . equipped in the spring a vessel of 130 lasts, called the Niew Nederlandt, whereof Cornelis Jacobsz Mey of Hoorn was skipper, with a company of 30 families, most Walloons, to plant a colony there. They sailed in the beginning of March, and directing their course by the Canary Islands, steered toward the Wild Coast, and gained the wind which luckily (took?) them in the beginning of May into the river called first *Rio De Montagnes*, now the river Mauritius,[1] lying in 40½ degrees."

Brodhead's account of what followed appears substantially correct. The yacht "Mackerel,"[2] having reached the mouth of the Hudson "pretty late" in the preceding December, was just at this time trading up the North River. When the "New Netherland" arrived, she found lying at anchor a French vessel, the captain of which was about to land for the purpose of setting up the standard of France and thereby claiming possession of the soil in the name of the most pious and Catholic King Louis. "But the Hollanders would not permit him," remarks the calm Wassenaer. In fact, to make their meaning quite clear, and just then receiving a timely reenforcement in the return of the "Mackerel" down the North River—they put two guns on a pinnace and therewith escorted the Frenchman clear out to

[1] The Hudson River.
[2] This, as we have seen, made part of the voyage in company with the "Pigeon", carrying De Forest to Guiana.

The De Forests and the

sea. Wassenaer says he repeated the experiment, but was "foiled in a similar manner."

Now there was clearly no Dutch settlement, garrison, or military power—no sort of official occupancy—at the mouth of the Hudson River, nor anywhere else in what is now the state of New York. Whatever was done in this matter was done by these Walloons in Mey's ship on their timely arrival. If the great Catholic power of France had definitely preëmpted this key of the New World, subsequent history would probably have been very different. And the coming of these Walloons was owing to the ambition, the perseverance, the leadership, of Jesse De Forest. As the relations become better recognized, it is probable that De Forest's name will be remembered as deserving a definite place, however modest, in American history.

B. PERSONNEL OF THE COLONY.—The original records of the West India Company were destroyed[1] about 1820, including all papers regarding the sailing of the New Netherland,[2] such as the manifest of cargo, list of passengers, and so on. In 1910 there were sold in Amsterdam five very important documents,[3] of recent discovery, evidently contemporaneous copies of original West India Company records. These give the full instructions sent over with Mey, as signed by three members of the Company under date of March, 1624.[4] No list of the

[1] Not by malice or accident, but officially.
[2] Brodhead.
[3] "A Walloon Family," p. 34.
[4] Further confirmation of the correct date.

Walloon Founding of New Amsterdam

colonists occurs here, and as the few records of the new settlement were unfortunately destroyed [1] within a short time after their landing by a "general conflagration," none has ever come to light. We know, however, that they formed a part of the band of would-be-emigrants recruited and enrolled by De Forest at the time of his application to Sir Dudley Carleton. It is certain that two of them were Philippe Du Trieux and his second wife, Susanna Du Chesne.[2] Their daughter Sara Du Trieux, who in 1641 married Isaac De Forest,[3] was born either just before or just after the landing of her parents. She may have been "the eldest child of New Amsterdam," though that person is generally supposed to be Sarah de Rapalye, born June 9, 1625, the daughter of Simon de Rapalye and his wife Catherine or Caterina Tricot. In spite of Caterina's conflicting memories at an advanced age, she and her husband are accepted by most as among the first comers.

Amid the very first records of New Amsterdam after the blank caused by the "general conflagration," we find many surnames identical with those upon the "Round Robin" presented by De Forest to Carleton. Besides those of De Forest and La Montagne, we may note the following duplicates: Cornille, Catoir, Campion, Damont, De Carpentier, De Croy, De Crenne, Du Four, De la Mot, Du Pon, De Trou, Gaspar, Ghiselin, Gille, Lambert, Le Roy,

---
[1] According to a letter written by Dominie Michaelius, the first pastor, on Aug. 11, 1628.
[2] Not Jacquemine Noiret, who died in Holland.
[3] Son of Jesse De Forest.

The De Forests and the Le Pou, Maton, and Martin. While this is scarcely proof that the groups of families were the same, it is certainly a striking coincidence, especially as there would be other like families whose names had no occasion to appear upon the records, and may fairly be considered as proof presumptive.

C. LANDING AT MANHATTAN; FIRST EXPERIENCES.—The little band bravely separated. One part remained on Manhattan Island; a larger one, consisting of some eighteen families, with Adriaen Joris as leader, settled at "Fort Orange";[1] some others, including four couples who had been married at sea, built "Fort Nassau" on the Delaware just below the site of Philadelphia, under the advice of Cornelis Mey; a few more even scattered out to the mouth of the "Fresh" or Connecticut River.[2] Still another little group betook themselves to a small bay or "bogt" on the west shore of Long Island, about opposite Corlaer's Hook on Manhattan, and but a little north of the spot where Breuckelen[3] was soon to rise. The name "Waalbogt"—the Walloons' Bay—survives in the term "Wallabout," still applied to the same locality. Says Brodhead,[4] "The descendants of the Walloons soon spread themselves over the country in the vicinity of the Waal-bogt, and the names of many of the most respectable families on Long Island to this day attest their French and Belgian origin."

[1] Presently known as Albany.
[2] This settlement, however, proved to be short-lived.
[3] Brooklyn.
[4] P. 154.

Walloon Founding of New Amsterdam

Like the "pères de familles" in Guiana, these colonists also sent back brave and cheerful word concerning the new land. "We were much charmed on arriving in this country," they reported.[1] Had the Dutch West India Company been sufficiently far-sighted in 1623 to transport fifty families to Guiana when besought to do so, and had it returned presently with cattle, implements, and comforts, as to the Hudson settlement, instead of marooning a few strong men in a far country, and neglecting its promises until the leader found an unknown grave, Holland might today have had a vast colonial empire in the New World south of the Isthmus of Panama.

As soon as the rude log forts were even partially completed, the colonists with good will "forthwith put the spade into the ground,"[2] according to Wassenaer, "and before the Mackerel sailed the grain was nearly as high as a man, so that they were bravely advanced."

D. COMPARATIVE HISTORIC IMPORTANCE OF THE LITTLE SETTLEMENT. — Here, again, is a point of importance. This was the first permanent, home-building, farming settlement in the present state of New York. The beginning here made was never abandoned or interrupted, but has steadily grown into the metropolis of the western world. And it was made by a picked band of Belgian-French Protestant refugees, recruited, held together through

[1] N. Y. Col. Doc. IV, p. 131.
[2] N. Y. Hist. Doc. Vol. IV, p. 132.

The De Forests and the many disappointments, and launched by that indefatigable Walloon, Jesse De Forest of Avesnes.

IX. Expedition of Jean La Montagne, De Forest's Colleague and Son-in-law, to Tobago

A. La Montagne's Return From the Guiana Expedition, and Marriage to Rachel De Forest. —When Dr. La Montagne returned to Leyden from the Guiana expedition, he reentered the University, and became one of the household of De Forest's widow, then living on the Voldergraft. A year later he married the young daughter of the house, Rachel De Forest. Apparently one adventure in colonization had but whetted La Montagne's appetite for more; since fifteen months after his marriage we find him sailing with his wife and baby on the "Fortuyn," commanded by his old friend Gelyn van Stapels, with some sixty odd other colonists bound for the island of Tobago.[1] On the way out, at St. Vincent, they met[2] two men who were the sole survivors of a colony sent out by the West India Company to Guiana, under one Jan van Ryen, only a year after the return of the survivors of the colony under De Forest which the Company had allowed to come to naught. Captain Jan van Ryen, lacking De Forest's tact and probably his fair dealing, had provoked the hitherto well-disposed natives into killing him and scattering his settlement.

[1] One of the Windward Islands, northwest of Guiana.
[2] Annual Report of West India Company.

Walloon Founding of New Amsterdam

B. UNSUCCESSFUL COLONY AT TOBAGO.—La Montagne remained at Tobago about five years; but, to be brief, at the end of three he found it necessary to send his family back to Leyden; and after two more, finding it still impossible to safeguard their return, he sacrificed his interests upon the island and rejoined them in Holland. Four years after his departure,[1] this colony also was wiped out by Spaniards and Caribs.

C. LA MONTAGNE'S RETURN, AND READINESS FOR NEW VENTURES.—With a flexible mind finely able to adapt itself with equal interest to the wilderness or to civilization, Dr. La Montagne for a third time tranquilly pursued his studies at the University of Leyden until, in the course of a year or so, the "wanderlust" again seized him. His young wife also, having been comfortably reestablished for several years under her mother's roof, and having now the future of several sturdy little sons to consider, appears to have felt refreshed and equipped for further adventure, especially as two of her brothers were of the proposed party, and her uncle Gerard was counseling and financing it.

X. EMIGRATION OF JESSE DE FOREST'S THREE CHILDREN AND SON-IN-LAW

A. GERARD DE FOREST, BROTHER OF JESSE.—Gerard De Forest appears to have been a leading member of the French colony in Leyden. After Jesse

[1] 1633.

The De Forests and the

De Forest's departure in 1623, his brother Gerard, up to that time a "dyer in black," applied for and received permission to occupy the place and to transact the former business of Jesse, a "dyer in colors." Having few children of his own, he seems to have felt a strong affection and family responsibility toward the fourteen children of his brother Jesse. He had stood godfather to a number, and as chosen witness to La Montagne's marriage with his niece Rachel; had apparently stood by the widowed Marie du Cloux as a brother, and was now planning a future for her younger sons.

B. HENDRICK DE FOREST.—Of these, Henri—or, in the Dutch equivalent, Hendrick—next older than his sister Rachel La Montagne, had already had some experience as a sailor and pioneer to the New World. In June, 1629, the West India Company had issued a "Charter of Freedoms and Exemptions for patroons,[1] masters or private persons who will plant any colonies in, and send cattle to, New Netherland." Of these patroons Kiliaen van Rensselaer was perhaps the most prominent. In the Van Rensselaer Bowier Manuscripts, recently translated and ably edited by A. J. F. van Laer, the State Archivist at Albany, N. Y., we find Kiliaen van Renssalaer's letter-books from 1634 to 1643, the Log of the yacht Rensselaerswyck,[2] and many other important documents,[3] including numerous entries

---

[1] A patroon was one who agreed to plant in New Netherland "a colony of fifty souls," upwards of fifteen years old, within the space of four years.
[2] 1636-37.
[3] See "A Walloon Family," p. 63.

Walloon Founding of New Amsterdam

concerning Gerard De Forest and his nephew Hendrick. Among these is an account of the voyage in 1636 of the Rensselaerswyck, in which several of Jesse De Forest's children and grandchildren, and his son-in-law La Montagne, sailed to the New World.

C. THE SWANENDAEL COLONY.—Van Rensselaer, with several other patroons, including Johannes De Laet, the historian, and David De Vries, the sea-captain, had become interested in the whaling industry at Swanendael, on the west shore of Delaware Bay. On Dec. 19, 1631, the patroons engaged Hendrick De Forest to go to Swanendael and take command of the colony already planted under Houset. The voyage,[1] during which Hendrick De Forest acted as chaplain[2] and steward,[3] was long and eventful. Before the vessel arrived, the colony was wiped out by the Indians—"lamentably killed, whereby *they*,"[4] said the patroons coolly, "suffered incalculable damage."[5] De Vries then set about getting a cargo of salt at St. Martin. The patroons of Swanendael seem to have been rather shabby as regards their pay-roll, for some years later, during his own absence, De Forest had to get his uncle Gerard to sue them for the amount due him.[6]

D. THE RENSSELAERSWYCK EXPEDITION.— In 1636 Jesse De Forest's two sons, Hendrick and

[1]"Voyages from Holland to America," by David De Vries (passim).
[2]"Voorleezer."
[3]"Commis of the Victuals."
[4]i.e., the patroons.
[5]Van Rensselaer Bowier MSS., pp. 196, 240, 241.
[6]See "The Declaration of Hendrick De Forest" in the notarial records at Amsterdam, as given (translated) in "A Walloon Family," p. 352.

Isaac, aged thirty and twenty respectively, decided that the time was ripe to carry out their dead father's long-cherished and fixed desire to found a family home in the New World. Kiliaen van Rensselaer had previously planted a colony called Rensselaerswyck at Fort Orange on the Hudson, and he now wished to reenforce this settlement by sending over a ship with settlers, merchandise, cattle and tools. Kiliaen being cramped in purse, however, was glad to enter into a partnership with Gerard De Forest. In a private letter he says, "As the equipment of this ship ran too high for me I granted Gerrit de foreest a half interest in it."[1]

Among the Notarial Records of Amsterdam is the full contract[2] entered into by "Mr. Kiliaen van Rensselaer with his associates of the first part and Mr. Gerrit de Forest of Leyden with his associates of the second part," agreeing to divide equally almost every expense, and adding,

"For conveying the settlers and the merchandise for the colony the above-mentioned Rensselaer shall allow Gerrit de Forest and his associates to share the right which as Patroon of New Netherland he has by virtue of act 13 of the granted Freedoms . . ."[3]

On Sept. 25, 1636, the ship, not a large one, set sail from Amsterdam. The skipper was Jan Schellinger; the mate, Hendrick De Forest. Besides a crew of twelve men, there were thirty-eight of Van

[1] Van Rensselaer Bowier MSS., p. 328.
[2] "A Walloon Family," p. 352.
[3] This was not a permanent distinction or social privilege, but referred to sailing and traffic rights.

Walloon Founding of New Amsterdam

Rensselaer's colonists for the upper Hudson and fourteen in the De Forest party. Hendrick, newly married, had left his wife with her mother for a time; Isaac was a bachelor of twenty; the La Montagnes had with them their three sons, and a daughter was born before they landed. With them were friends and neighbors.

The surprising lack of judgment shown by most of these early colonial expeditions, in setting forth at the autumn equinoctial, had the usual results. The voyage was one of eventful hardship, most graphically set forth in the "Log of the Rensselaerswyck." Off Madeira they had a brush with a "Frenchman from New Rochelle," in preparation for which they "cleared away the chests and the cows[1] with which the deck was encumbered," but came away none the worse for the encounter. After going as far south as the Canaries, they caught the trade winds, and at last, on March 1, 1637, came in by "Godyn's Point,"[2] majestically escorted by a school of whales—"some ten or twenty swimming for about two hours about our ship." Four days later they dropped anchor "off the Manatans." As soon as the Walloons were landed, with their belongings, the yacht sailed on up the river to Fort Orange with Van Rensselaer's colonists and property.

E. LOCATION OF LANDS FIRST TAKEN UP BY THE DE FORESTS.—With the intention of raising tobacco, the De Forests soon selected a tract of fertile bottom-

---
[1] One wonders where these were bestowed.
[2] Sandy Hook.

land in the northern part of the island, called "Muscoota"—"the flat land"—by the Indians. Hendrick secured from van Twiller, the Director, a grant of a hundred "morgens" of land "between the hills and the kill that runs round the island." Maps of the time,[1] preserved in the New York Public Library, show this land to be between Morningside Heights and Harlem Creek,[2] running on the north to perhaps 124th Street, and on the south to include the high land in Central Park as far as 109th Street. Here he promptly put up a thatched house "42 feet long, with a brick chimney."[3]

F. DEATH OF HENDRICK DE FOREST.—Many papers of importance concerning these early colonists were wholly lost in the fire which destroyed the archives of the State Capitol at Albany in 1911, but the scattered, incomplete records contain much of interest. Hendrick, still "mate and trader" of the Rensselaerswyck, was called upon, when she returned from her three months' stay at Fort Orange, to sail with her to Virginia. As his brother Isaac, being under the age of twenty-five, was by Dutch law still a minor, Hendrick left his "Muscoota bouwery," with other business interests, in charge of his brother-in-law, Dr. La Montagne. On the Virginia voyage Hendrick De Forest contracted "the epidemical disease,"[4] then very malignant, and on July 26, 1637, ten days after the yacht's return to New Amsterdam,

[1] Reproduced by Innes and Mrs. de Forest.
[2] Col. Doc. Vol. XIV, p. 11.
[3] Most of the chimneys were of the "catstick and daub" variety.
[4] Van Rensselaer Bowier MSS., "The Log of the Rensselaerswyck," p. 382.

Walloon Founding of New Amsterdam

Captain Chellinger entered on his log, "About two o'clock in the morning my mate heindrick de Freest died."

Again within a year, La Montagne was called upon to bury a De Forest who had sought with him to found a colony in the New World. In each case, daring had been rewarded only by disaster and death; in each case, also, a widow in Leyden was to learn of her loss long afterwards.

XI. THE "MUSCOOTA BOUWERIES," OR WALLOON FARMSTEADS

A. HENDRICK DE FOREST'S, LATER LA MONTAGNE'S.—Hendrick De Forest's holding was for some time honestly and ably managed by Dr. La Montagne, who presently made a satisfactory accounting to the widow, Gertrude Bornstra,[1] who had remained in Leyden. Before very long she made a second marriage with Andries Hudde,[2] who found Hendrick's American property worth emigrating to claim as his inheritance. The deed signed by Director Kieft on July 20, 1638, giving to Andries Hudde the two hundred acres which had been Hendrick De Forest's, is the first legal conveyance of land recorded on Manhattan Island.[3]

La Montagne presently bought this property for 1800 guilders, and named it in hope "Vredendael"—

[1] Van Rensselaer Bowier MSS., p. 382.
[2] According to an odd, almost Scriptural custom of the times, Gertrude named Hudde's first child, born five years after De Forest's death, and upon its death, even their second child, born two years later, after her former husband Hendrick De Forest, "that his name might not die out in the land."
[3] N. Y. Colonial Documents, Vol. XIV, p. 11.

The De Forests and the Peace Valley or Peaceful Dale. As we shall see, the hope embodied in this name was to fall sadly short of realization. On this estate a beautiful flowing spring was soon called "Montagne's Fountain." This spring, still bearing the same name, has survived, and may today be seen flowing in a rippling stream with waterfalls until it empties into Harlem Mere in Central Park.[1]

B. ISAAC DE FOREST'S HOLDING.—Isaac de Forest, a young man of twenty-one at his landing in 1637, at first aided his brother Hendrick to improve the latter's bouwery. Upon Hendrick's death, Isaac turned to similar services for his sister Rachel and her husband, with whom for some time he made his home; but in the meantime he also secured his own holding of land. This was a strip of about a hundred acres,[2] nearly a mile in length, beginning on Harlem Creek opposite Hendrick's land,[3] and running eastward to the shore of the Hellegat,[4] opposite Bronck's Kill.[5] Settlers, at this period, appear to have been little more than "squatters" recognized by the Company, which required only that the land be cultivated and improved within two years, and that after ten years' free use the settlers should annually tithe their crops [6] to the Company. Formal titles appear to have been "confirmed" by successive directors.

[1]Photograph in "A Walloon Family," p. 105.
[2]"Map of Nieuwe Haerlem Village Plots," 1670, in Riker's "History of Harlem," p. 260.
[3]Later known as "Vredendael."
[4]The Harlem River.
[5]About First Avenue and 126th St.
[6]That is, hand over ten per cent.

Walloon Founding of New Amsterdam

In time, of course, permanent papers were held by the grantees.

Isaac planted his land to tobacco until his coming of age, when he at once married,[1] and built a dwelling upon it. He engaged two English carpenters to make him a substantial house, eighteen by thirty feet, "with two four-light windows and two three-light windows," "tight all round" against the weather; a separate kitchen, sixteen by twenty feet, covered with clapboards and furnished with an "English chimney" made of cobblestone; also a tobacco-house sixty feet long, with "inside work." For these buildings[2] he paid three hundred Carolus guilders, or $160. To meet such bills he had something from several tobacco crops, together with part of 164 guilders left him jointly with his brother Jan from Hendrick's estate.

The young couple lived upon this grant of land for a year or more, until, as the danger from the savages became imminent, the young man decided to take his wife and baby into town for greater safety. He leased his bouwery to John Denton for three years[3] and at once moved closer in. Denton was to take possession in October; but before that date tomahawks were out in such force[4] that the new tenant refused to begin residence. De Forest's tilled fields and new farmstead were laid waste.[5] As hold-

---
[1] As the bride, Sara du Trieux, is entered on the church records as "young girl of New Netherland," she was evidently not born in Leyden; and as her parents landed in the spring of 1624, she could not at this time have been more than seventeen. She may have been born on the voyage, or among the first children.
[2] N. Y. Col. MSS., Vol. I, p. 250.   [3] July 6, 1643.
[4] N. Y. Col. MSS., p. 117.   [5] This was the time when Montagne lost Vredendael.

The De Forests and the

ings of this sort were perforce deserted during the time the savages were on the war path, the owners thought it safer[1] to take out new "land briefs." Montagne's new patent was signed by Director Kieft on May 9, 1647, two days before his embarkation on a return voyage to Holland; while only six days later, De Forest's was issued by the new Governor, Stuyvesant.[2]

By 1650 it was supposed that a permanent peace with the savages had been established. De Forest sold most of his property at this place to William Beeckman, a well-known early burgher of the growing town.[3] Three years later Beeckman sold it to Claesen Swits, who within two years[4] was murdered there, his family carried off by the Indians, and his farmstead destroyed. This was the occasion of the Directors' forbidding isolated dwellings. They ordered laid out a village wherein the surviving settlers might gather for mutual defense and common safety. Isaac De Forest's land, being well situated, well cleared, and easily accessible from "the Hellegat,"[5] was chosen as the site. Here in 1658 was located the village of Nieuwe Haerlem, with Isaac's wagon-track or farm lane for its one first street. This, of course, in time grew to be a city in itself, until merged in Greater New York. De Forest and La Montagne had had enough of the Muscoota region; they were too safe, and too well occupied, in New Amsterdam,

[1] Or perhaps it was legally necessary.
[2] Calendar of Dutch MSS., p. 375.
[3] N. Y. Col. MSS., p. 46.
[4] Sept., 1655.
[5] The Harlem River.

Walloon Founding of New Amsterdam

to resume residence at or near the new village. La Montagne's son Jan, however, was one of the first householders, and for long a leading citizen of New Haerlem.

Isaac and Sara De Forest lived first in New Amsterdam on the "Marckveldt," or market square,[1] just outside the fort, and divided from it by a narrow lane called Winkel Straet. A little later he moved into a better house on Brouwer Straet, or the Brewers' Street, so named because the great brewery of the West India Company was the most notable building upon it. De Forest himself was by this time a brewer on a large scale. This street De Forest and some others presently paved at their own expense; it has ever since been called Stone Street, being the first paved way in the city.

At the time the records begin,[2] the holding of Philippe du Trieux was on high ground near the East River,[3] overlooking "Smit's Vly."[4] At the time of his daughter Sara's marriage to Isaac De Forest he was living nearer the center of the settlement in a house which he had built on "Bever Graft."[5] This is now the site of Fulton Market.

C. GENERAL CONDITIONS.—Something may be added regarding the general conditions of life in the colony. In 1643 Director Kieft told Father Jogues, the Jesuit missionary to the Indians, that there were

[1] Maps and plans in Innes; also Calendar of Dutch MSS., p. 370.
[2] Perhaps earlier, of course.
[3] Maps in N. Y. Public Library.
[4] Still called "The Swamp."
[5] Beaver Street.

at that time "four or five hundred men of different sects and nations" living in or close to New Amsterdam,[1] and that eighteen different languages were spoken. Mrs. de Forest quotes from Madam Knight's "Brief Description of New York," as follows:

"The Buildings are Brick generally, very stately & high. The Bricks in some of the Houses are of divers Coullers and laid in Checkers, being glazed, look very agreeable. The inside of them is neat to admiration."[2] The doors of most of the houses were "equally divided as in Holland with an upper & a lower half"; "the gable ends of the high roofs were notch'd like steps."[2] Both Dutch and Belgian-French seem to have taken great satisfaction in the cheap abundance of building materials. Many supplies and comforts, of course, were still shipped from the Old World; the colonists, however, appear to have been both industrious and ingenious in the local production of property and merchandise.

"The Huguenot refugees," says the author of "French Blood in America,"[3] "were gentle, trained in many arts, and possessed of the keen perceptions, the courtesy, and the easy adaptability of their race. . . . Tradition says that the first to utilize the remnants of worn-out garments by cutting them into strips and weaving them into carpets were the French. The rag carpet was in its day an advance agent of comfort and culture. . . . Among the

[1] "Narratives of New Netherland," by J. F. Jameson, p. 259.
[2] "A Walloon Family," p. 119.
[3] "French Blood in America," by Lucian J. Fosdick, pp. 406 et seq.

Walloon Founding of New Amsterdam

earliest importations of the French settlers were the spinning-wheels and looms of better quality than were previously known here. . . . Where the English and Dutch dyed linen yarn of heavy quality and wove it into ugly stripes and checks for bed and window curtains, the French[1] used either white linen or that with but one color, dainty shades of light blue or dusky green or a subdued gold colour, made by dyes of which they had brought the secret with them, being preferred. . . . The cultivated taste and the dainty arts brought from France made the homes of the Huguenots much more attractive in appearance than those of the other colonists, even though the latter might have far more wealth."

De Forest and Du Trieux[2] are the only dyers noted. Their skill perhaps served all.

Men servants, skilled workmen and ordinary laborers were more easily to be found than women servants. On emigrating, the young De Forests had been prudent enough to engage and bring with them two stout men, Tobias Teunissen and Willem Frederick Bout, under contract to serve for three years after landing.[3] Their sister, young Mrs. La Montagne, however, with four little children at first and presently more, and a household including her two brothers and these two serving men, besides her husband, could find no domestic aid until a man-servant Ariean was engaged at twelve and a half florins per month. The Rev. Jonas Michaelius, the first Dutch

[1] Fosdick, p. 406 et seq.
[2] A worsted-dyer from Roubaix, near Avesnes.
[3] Van Rensselaer Bowier, MSS., p. 360.

The De Forests and the

minister sent to the colony, soon after wrote home, "Maid servants are not here to be had, at least none whom they can advise me to take; and the Angola slave women thievish, lazy and useless trash."[1]

The tobacco plantations were largely worked by negro slaves, either privately owned by the individual settlers, or hired from the West India Company. The Directors of the Company encouraged private expeditions to "buy"[2] slaves on the Guinea Coast. They "granted liberty to particular merchants to send two or three ships to the coast of Africa to purchase slaves, & to promote the settlement of the country by importing the same."[2] These, of course, were mostly men, not relieving the problem of domestic service. Isaac De Forest was a slave-holder, but he finally sent to Holland for a house-servant, paying all the expenses of her passage. Here, however, he caught a Tartar, for she "sought to get out of the house as soon as she was in it, abusing him and his wife very spitefully."[3]

Others had similar experiences. Home making laid heavy burdens upon the pioneer mothers, struggling single-handed with the problems of ceaseless household toil and the simultaneous rearing of large families. Doubtless many another, like Rachel De Forest, succumbed at thirty-three or thirty-four, leaving a spotless home, six young children, several little graves, and a husband soon to be consoled, like

[1] Letter of Michaelius, in N. Y. Col. Doc., Vol. II, p. 768.
[2] N. Y. Col. Doc., XIV, p. 209.
[3] Records of New Amsterdam, Vol. II, pp. 350, 351.

Walloon Founding of New Amsterdam

so many of our egoist forefathers, who complacently prided themselves upon the large families for which they were indebted, on the average, to the joint efforts of three wives apiece—successively, of course, in so highly-civilized a country as ours.

D. DANGER FROM THE INDIANS.—Danger from the savages was for a long time acute. Massacres occurred here as elsewhere. The local government even made regulations forbidding settlers to establish isolated homesteads. For a number of years La Montagne was Chief Military Officer, leading expeditions in person and laying all possible plans for the defense of the colony. This was no light responsibility.

When the new Director-General, William Kieft, reached New Amsterdam in March, 1638, he was empowered to select his own councillors. He chose only one, and that one Dr. La Montagne, "a proper experienced person." Kieft and La Montagne, then, for a long time *were* the Council—no others being added. Kieft was warlike, determined upon exterminating the Indians; La Montagne saw this as reckless folly. Kieft persisted, and on Feb. 25, 1643,[1] slaughtered a number of Indians. Naturally they retaliated. The result of Kieft's foolhardiness nearly destroyed the whole colony. The Indians killed every settler they could find. Scarcely one remained on Manhattan Island except in New Amsterdam.[2] Montagne's prosperous bouwery at Vred-

[1] Calendar of Dutch MSS., p. 84.
[2] History of Harlem, by Riker.

The De Forests and the

endael was wiped out, Montagne losing everything that he was unable to carry away.

In the late autumn of the same year [1] a touching appeal for aid was despatched by the colonists to the West India Company.[2] A condensed extract follows:

"On the island of the Manachatas, from the north even unto the Fresh Water [3] there are no more than five or six spots inhabited at this date. . . . We have no other shelter remaining for ourselves, our wives and children, than around and adjoining Fort Amsterdam at the Manahactas. The fort is defenceless and entirely out of order, and resembles (with submission) rather a mole-hill than a fort against an an enemy. . . . The population is composed mainly of women and children; the freemen (exclusive of the English) are about 200 strong, who must protect by force their families now skulking in straw huts outside the Fort. . . . We turn then to your Honors; we humbly pray and beseech you to be pleased to help us in this distressed plight, so that this place and all of us, with wives and children, may not be delivered over a prey to these cruel heathen." [4]

Their Honors, however, both stingy and hard of heart, afforded no relief. The West India Company seem ever to have had "the souls of shopkeepers" in any question of reenforcing or defending a colony

[1] Oct. 24, 1643.
[2] Col. Doc., p. 190.
[3] From the Hudson River to the Connecticut.
[4] Col. Doc., p. 190.

Walloon Founding of New Amsterdam

they had once established. A second petition,[1] equally despairing, was addressed to the States General at The Hague. This (in part) said:

"We, wretched people, must skulk, with wives and children that still survive, in poverty together, in and around the fort at the Manahatas where we are not safe even for an hour whilst the Indians daily threaten to overwhelm us. Very little can be planted this autumn, and much less in the spring; so that it will come to pass that all of us who will yet save our lives must of necessity perish next year of hunger and sorrow unless our God have pity on us."[2]

No aid was afforded by Holland. It was clear that war with the savages was not to be averted. La Montagne was made "General" of the united Dutch, Walloon, and English forces.[3] Continuing to hold this position, he headed many expeditions against the Indians, and successfully defended the little settlement, until in the summer of 1645, the red men, apparently tired out, concluded a peace which it was hoped might prove permanent.

When Peter Stuyvesant landed[4] as the new Director-General, he at once retained La Montagne as a member of his council, so that the subsequent records contain frequent references to "Councillor La Montagne" as one of the most influential men of New Amsterdam. In 1655 the armed savages suddenly appeared before Manhattan in a fleet of sixty-four

[1] Nov. 3, 1643.
[2] N. Y. Col. Doc. I, p. 139.
[3] N. Y. Col. MSS., p. 186.
[4] May, 1647.

The De Forests and the

canoes. The ensuing scenes were very bloody. Again many of the whites, like Kieft, were for a war of extermination; but La Montagne, realizing the weakness of the little colony, again pleaded peace counsels; and once more the village escaped. Next year, the difficulties with the Indians proving still acute and increasingly threatening, he was made Vice-Director at Fort Orange.[1] The same year he was one of two men[2] to sign the treaty of sale with the Indians for the territory on the Schuylkill.[3] A few years later,[4] while he was still living at Fort Orange, his daughter Rachel, the wife of Surgeon Gysbert Van Imbroech of Esopus, was carried away, with her little daughter, Lysbet, by the Indians, and only La Montagne's personal reputation among the savages finally secured their release unharmed.[5]

La Montagne appears to have had a gift for getting on peaceably with the natives, similar to that which Jesse De Forest showed in Guiana. We have seen that when the latter died, he was "deeply regretted" by the natives, who had taken a great liking to him; while his successor, in spite of the friendly relation opened by De Forest, at once so alienated the savages that he and his colony soon perished.

La Montagne appears as one of the most courageous, efficient and public-spirited citizens of New Amsterdam. His personal property and interests seem to have been wholly sacrificed in his defense of

[1] Albany on the Hudson.
[2] L. van Dincklage being the other
[3] N. Y. Col. Doc., p. 593.
[4] 1663.
[5] N Y Col. Doc. XIII, pp. 246, 271, 273.

Walloon Founding of New Amsterdam

the settlement against the Indians. His latter days were weary, sad, and harried by failing fortunes. In 1662, being then nearly seventy, he wrote to Stuyvesant and the council at New Amsterdam a rather touching letter, saying in part,

"I always kept my household in victuals and clothes here as temperately as a common burgher;[1] but the excessive dearth of all things has driven me insensibly into such need and poverty, as that never in the 68 years that I have lived, so great distress have I felt, finding myself destitute of all means to provide for my daily bread, and provisions for the winter."[2]

In 1664, New Netherland passed into English hands. La Montagne drops out of sight. He may have returned to Holland with Stuyvesant. I do not find note of his death.

XII. Place Held by the Walloons in the Early Years of New Amsterdam

A. Civic Organization.—In the early days of New Amsterdam, the civic organization was much like that of a modern city, with similar officials under different names. The Director-General, commonly called the "Governor," held at first the place of Mayor. His Councillors, few or many at his choice, were appointed by himself. There was thus a decided centralization of power in the chief magistrate. As the authority of the Director-General, however, extended over all New Netherland, the city govern-

---
[1] He was still Vice-Director at Fort Orange.
[2] Riker's History of Harlem, p. 794.

ment as such soon became more definitely organized. After Kieft's obstinacy in forcing an issue with the Indians had such disastrous results, he was ready to allow some local aid and cooperation in the management of the colony. In 1643 he invited the "Commonalty of the Manhattans" to elect some six or eight of their number as an advisory board. These formed the "Eight Men," later the "Nine Men," as they were called; they attended court, acted as referees and advisers, and when asked, expressed their opinion upon any matter in which the Governor and his Council saw fit to consult them. In 1653, again, a decided change occurred. The city being incorporated, the Nine Men gave way to a court of magistrates consisting of a schout or mayor, two burgomasters, and five schepens. "Small burghers" were something like ordinary members of a modern Commercial Club, especially in one where the membership is not cheapened by over-solicitation; and the "Great Burghers" were more, perhaps, like chairmen of the leading committees of a Commercial Club or Board of Trade. All city offices, even minor ones, were much more guarded in respect to eligibility, taken with more serious sense of responsibility, and in general indicated either a higher social standing, or greater dignity of character, than is commonly the case in modern civic affairs. To be either a "Small Burgher" or a "Great Burgher," the privileged party must "take up his abode here in New Netherland three consecutive years, and in addition build in this city, New Amsterdam, a

Walloon Founding of New Amsterdam

decent citizen dwelling," "continuously maintain fire and light therein"; and, in addition, be chosen by the city authorities, take an oath of fidelity to the city, pay the prescribed fees, and be duly registered. The nucleus of the first list was made up *ex officio* of the Governor and Council, the clergy, the commissioned officers in the city regiment, and, by an unblushing "grandfather clause," their sons and sons-in-law as well.

B. REPRESENTATIVE WALLOON CITIZENS.—Cornelis Mey of Hoorn, the skipper engaged to take over De Forest's colony of emigrants, remained with them as "director" for the first year. After him Willem van Hulst, a man of little force, served for a time; then, in response to the desire of the Walloon colony, a man of their own blood, faith, and language [1] was sent out as director—Peter Minuit,[2] son of Jean and Sara Minuit, Walloon refugees to the Huguenot colony at Wesel.[3] Oddly enough, while no one appears to have considered the Pilgrim Fathers of Plymouth a Dutch colony because they sailed from Leyden, yet it has been assumed that the Belgian-French colony, sailing at the same time from the same place, were Hollanders. It is true that the first sailed in a ship called the "Mayflower," under auspices of the "Virginia Company," while the latter embarked in a vessel called the "New Netherland,"

[1]Letters of Michaelius (1628) in N. Y. Col. Doc., Vol. II. Article by Rev. J. G. Sardemann of Wesel, in Dawson's Hist. Magazine for April, 1868. Statement of Harless, State Archivist of Dusseldorf, in N. Y. Gen. and Biog. Record for Oct., 1895. [2]Appleton's Dict. of Am. Biog.
[3]On the lower Rhine, not far from either France or the Netherlands.

The De Forests and the

chartered by the West India Company; yet it was but through a disappointment to earnest efforts that the Walloons had not come through arrangements made with the English corporation—in which case, presumably, they would long have been classed as British emigrants. At all events, the greater part of the first settlers of Manhattan have been but recently perceived to be French Protestants; and it may still be news to some that the first real Governor [1] was also one, being born in a Walloon colony of French parents,[2] and a deacon in the Walloon Church at Wesel until the year before his appointment to the New Netherlands. It is probable that his surname is properly the French "Minuit"—midnight—and no more rightly "Minnewit" than "Du Trieux" is properly "Truax," or Molyneux "Monlux," though both of these family names have been so spelled and so pronounced.

If Minuit's nationality has been mistaken, there has been no such error in regard to his services. At the time of his arrival the little settlements were in sore danger from the savages, who were even indulging in cannibalism. At least they wholly made way thus with one Tyman Bouwensz, "after they had well cooked him."[3] Minuit speedily made a peace, never broken, with the Mohawks,[4] concentrated his settlements on Manhattan, and before five months were ended had bought peaceably from

[1] Though technically the third "Director."
[2] Appleton's Dict. of Am. Biog.
[3] N. Y. Col. Doc. Vol. III. Extracts from Wassenaer.
[4] The recent feasters.

Walloon Founding of New Amsterdam

the Indians the entire island of Manhattan, more than 22,000 acres, for sixty guilders—less than twenty-five dollars. Even when turned out of office a few years later, when the Dutch outnumbered the Walloons, he organized, promoted, and successfully planted the colony of New Sweden on the eastern coast of Delaware.

In the State Papers at Albany, such as the Register of the Provincial Secretary; in the Aldermanic Records of New Amsterdam in the City Hall, New York, and in the printed records of New York City, such as the list of office-holders from O'Callaghan's New Netherland Register, are to be found scores, perhaps hundreds, of entries indicating the position and services of the Walloon citizens of New Amsterdam. In the Appendix to J. W. De Forest's single volume, "The De Forests of Avesnes," appears a copious selection of entries concerning the De Forest family and those closely connected with them by marriage, such as the Du Trieux and La Montagnes, De Riemers and Van Imbroecks. Many others are to be found in the Year Books of the Holland Society of New York, the "Documentary History of the State of New York," and the "New York Historical Collections," as well as in the quarterly publications of the "New York Genealogical and Biographical Society." In the "New York Historical Society Collections" for 1885, also, is a very interesting and illuminating article of some length, by Mrs. Robert De Lancey, on "Burghers and Freemen of New York."

The De Forests and the

In the first list issued of "Those who have the Burgher Right Pursuant to Privilege,"[1] the name of Johannes La Montagne heads the list for the "Great Burgher Right," and that of Isaac De Forest the one for the lesser privilege.[2] Not long afterward, Governor Stuyvesant, having "taken into serious consideration and reflection the small number of Great Burghers" . . . "found it advantageous for this city to increase the said number of Great Burghers and to reenforce it with six old and suitable persons." One of these was Isaac De Forest, presently referred to as "one of the most influential burghers and inhabitants of the city."[3] Five days later he was also elected "Schepen"—a coveted honor at this time.

Naturally, he had before this held creditably many minor offices. In 1652 he was one of the Nine Men; in 1653, city inspector of tobacco; in 1656, Schepen, and inspector of weights and measures; in 1658, again Schepen, and asks to be relieved of the superintendence of the Brewer's Street. He seems to have been much in demand[4] as "Orphanmaster"—that is, guardian of the children whose parents had been killed by the Indians, or other minors. Often he is on record as ransoming children held by the savages; often appointed administrator, arbitrator, holder of trust funds, or given power of attorney in interests of importance.

[1] Dated April 10, 1657.
[2] The Small Burgher Right.
[3] "Records of New Amsterdam," Vol. II, p. 315.
[4] Extracts from Dutch Documents in Year-Book of the Holland Society for 1900, pp. 112, 117, 121, etc. Twenty or more De Forest entries.

Walloon Founding of New Amsterdam

Judging from the entries of his foreign shipments, he seems also to have been one of the leading brewers and tobacco merchants. He owned a number of houses, loaned money, bought a tract of land on Long Island, dealt in furs, owned boats, entered into various business firms. Innes gives [1] "Isaac De Forest . . . a prominent place in the early history of New Netherland." By the records he is shown to be a public-spirited man. When Stuyvesant [2] asked for voluntary subscriptions to repair and strengthen the town's outer walls, he was one of the first to respond. In 1653 he was among twenty - one prominent citizens who offered and promised the burgomasters and schepens to pay certain extra taxes "for paying the public expenses and keeping in repair the works" of the little city.[3] As previously mentioned, he was one of the property owners on Brouwer Straet to offer to pave it at their own expense "with round stones," furnishing both the material and the labor.[4] Once he was assessed a hundred florins "for the defense of the city," no one else being assessed more than two hundred. In 1664 he was spoken of as "one of the most affluent inhabitants of the city."

Yet at his death he was not a wealthy man, his estate being valued only at some 15,000 florins. He had lived honorably and as became a man of public

---
[1] "Amsterdam and Its People," by J. H. Innes, Ch. VIII, pp. 71-74.
[2] In passing it might be noted that the wife of Peter Stuyvesant, most Dutch of men, was a Walloon; so also was his sister's husband. Stuyvesant's descendants are half Walloon at the outset.
[3] "Records of New Amsterdam," Vol. I, pp. 67, 127.
[4] Ibid, p. 300.

spirit; he had brought up a large family;[1] he had been administrator of the estate and guardian of the children of both his brother-in-law and his father-in-law; and he had repeatedly furnished ransom for the piteous little orphans held captive in savage hands. On the whole, he had probably done something better with his money than hoarding it, when in the summer of 1674 he died at the rather early age of fifty-six.

His wife, Sara Du Trieux,[2] survived him without remarriage some eighteen years, living quietly in the Brouwer Straet house. Their eight sons, all of whom had been taught some useful occupation, in course of time scattered as to their place of residence, but all prospered in worldly affairs and in a reputation for being upright, public-spirited men. The De Forests in America now number uncounted thousands, all descendants of Jesse and Isaac De Forest, and all, so far as known, intelligent and useful citizens, serving the state wherever their lot falls. Their names are thick on the alumni rolls of the best colleges; the "De Forest scholarships" and "The De Forest prize" at Yale are among her coveted distinctions. Despite exile, poverty, sorrow and disappointment, and his own lonely, lost grave beside the Wyapoko, the eager dream and hope of Jesse De Forest of Avesnes, that he might safely and permanently establish his family in the New World, has been fully realized.

[1] Eight sons and a daughter survive him.
[2] Or Sarah Philips, as she is called in the Dutch records to indicate the name of her father, Philippe Du Trieux.

Walloon Founding of New Amsterdam

The services of Dr. La Montagne, the first physician of the colony, for a long time the Governor's only Councillor, and the wise Commander-in-chief, against the savages, of the united Dutch, English and Walloon forces, have already been noted. No extended account has been given of Philippe Du Trieux, De Forest's father-in-law. He was one of the first ship-load of settlers, and for a long time "Court Marshal" of New Netherland. De Trous, Trows, Truells, and Truaxes of today, as well as a few who still maintain the older name in uncorrupted form, are, for the most part, the descendants of Philippe Du Trieux and his wife Susanna Du Chesne. Some of the surnames of this little colony have entirely disappeared in modern life, some have so altered as to be scarcely recognizable, some are still evident in large numbers. So far as visible surname is concerned, a deal of good blood disappears by marriage in each generation; yet it is hardly to be doubted that the qualities of this old Huguenot stock have come down by the distaff side as well as by that of the spear. Their dear-bought freedom of conscience; their intention of good citizenship; their hardy physique and industry; their warm affections, "answerable courages," and skill in the joy of living, are doubtless working for good, though unrecognized, in later generations.

C. IMPORTANT CONTRIBUTIONS TO THE EARLY LIFE OF THE COLONY.—But apart from this probability, if we look back dispassionately at the unquestioned early actions of these first-comers, there appear to be several worth recounting, when we pause to consider how differently history might have developed along the North Atlantic seaboard, had these pioneers been absent or of a different sort. First may be noted the driving out by De Forest's Walloon colony, on their arrival at Manhattan in 1624, of the French commander about to land for the purpose of setting up the arms of France, then a strongly Catholic power. Second, the establishment, by this same French Protestant band, of the first permanent, crop-raising, town-building settlement, never since destroyed or abandoned, upon the soil that later became the State of New York, and upon the site of the greatest city in the western hemisphere. Third, the purchase of the island of Manhattan from the Indians by Minuit upon his arrival in 1626. Fourth, the treaty of La Montagne with the sachems for the purchase of all the territory on the Schuylkill River. Lastly, at a critical time, after many massacres, the successful defense of the little colony against the Indians by a combined force of Walloons, English and Dutch under command of Jean La Montagne. All these are surely events of moment in the early history of both the metropolis and the commonwealth.

XIII. Conclusion: Investigation of the Facts by the Holland Society of New York

Some years ago the Holland Society of New York, a social and patriotic organization whose chief qualification for membership is direct descent in the male

Walloon Founding of New Amsterdam

line from one or more early Dutch settlers, began to be assailed by doubts regarding the priority of their claim to being descended from the first founders of New Amsterdam—a confidence in which, with a pleasant pride, they had long reposed. The gathering evidence contrary to this supposition, and the ensuing discussions, presently caused a delegation of the members to visit the city of Leyden on a mission of special research. The result of this and of further inquiry appears in the Year Book of the Holland Society for 1895, in an article as follows:[1]

"Jesse De Forest or Peter Minuit? Facts from Leyden going to show that the former was the founder of New Amsterdam.

"A letter from George W. Van Siclen, a prominent officer of the Holland Society, says: . . " 'Possessing some information on that subject myself, I still thought it best to write to Mr. Charles M. Dozy, Archivist of Leyden, and inquire into the historical facts. I have just received his answer, which I send herewith.

" 'When the delegation of the Holland Society of New York visited Holland in 1888, a most elaborate display of old maps, books, engravings and original MSS. was prepared for us at Leyden, and I had in my hand the original minutes of the City Council of Leyden, dated Aug. 27, 1622, granting permission to Jesse De Forest to enroll the Walloon colonists. (Also the original MS. poll-tax list, giving names, localities, and assessments of William Brewster, John

[1] Year Book of the Holland Society for 1895, p. 121.

The De Forests and the

Robinson and the other Pilgrim Fathers while they were living in Leyden in 1622.)
GEORGE W. VAN SICLEN.
New York, March 13, 1895.'"

The letter from Mr. Dozy follows:
". . . You ask my opinion about the founding of New York. You are right in thinking that the question does interest me, as I made researches about Jesse De Forest at Avesnes and Sedan.

"Minuit was the third Governor of the colony; he organized the administration; he made a treaty with the Indians that rendered the Dutch proprietors of the whole island instead of possessors only by right of first discovery or occupation; he fortified the settlement that had already existed three years. His importance for the colony should not be disregarded, but before his directorship, since 1623, there was a settlement on Manhattan Island that had already received important accessions from Holland, with a supply of live stock and farming tools.

"Jesse De Forest, born at Avesnes between 1570 and 1580, living in 1601 and 1608 at Sedan, and 1605 at Leyden, had applied in the name of fifty-six Walloon families, who wished to go to Virginia, to the ambassador of England at The Hague. . . . In August, 1622, Jesse sent a petition to the States-General of the United Provinces, asking to be allowed to enroll Protestant families for emigration. . . . The permission was given, the ship was equipped, and in March, 1623, the *New Netherland* left the

Walloon Founding of New Amsterdam

Dutch shores. In May the mouth of the River Hudson was reached. One division of the colonists went on and built Fort Orange, the origin of the present Albany. But the other part settled on Manhattan Island and the name Walenboght or Walloon Bay, the Wallabout of today, bears testimony to their being Walloons. It cannot be denied that from that fact, from the arrival of the New Netherland in May, 1623, dates the permanent occupation of the site of New York.

"It was Jesse who had written the address to England, and who was the advocate of the would-be colonists before the Ambassador; it was Jesse who had given the impulse to the expedition by his petition to the States, and had enrolled the emigrants. . . . As there is no doubt that the first permanent settlement on Manhattan dates from May, 1623,[1] the fact that Jesse De Forest prepared and organized that colonization[2] and was almost certainly the leader of it, gives him a right to be called the founder of New Amsterdam.

Charles M. Dozy."

The manful publication of these papers by the disappointed Holland Society adds weight to the evidence, such as was afforded when John Robinson's bitter enemies admitted that he was "the most learned, polished and modest spirit that ever separated from the Church of England."

[1] It will be noticed that Mr. Dozy, though one of the careful authorities, still gives 1623 as the correct date of landing. This was before the discovery and publication of De Forest's Journal, as previously noted.

[2] See previous pages.

Walloon Founding of New Amsterdam

Plans for the tercentenary of the founding of New York City are already under way. In this every effort toward accuracy will doubtless be made, judging from the researches and tentative plans already being made. In the New York Genealogical and Biographical Record for January, 1914,[1] is published an article of some length upon Philippe Du Trieux, which closes with the following words:

"The earlier history of Philippe Du Trieux confirms the historical data which have led historians of the New Netherland to place the first settlement of that colony in 1624, and to ascribe to a company of Walloons who came thither in that year under the leadership of Jesse De Forest the honor of being the first citizens of what is now New York. In 1924, when the State of New York celebrates its three hundredth anniversary as a European settlement, Jesse De Forest and his little band of exiled Walloons will be found to lead the long procession of emigrants who for one reason or another have made the New World their resting-place. And of the few of this early company who settled on Manhattan Island, Philippe Du Trieux, because of his now full record, may claim special consideration."

1924 is now a milestone not far ahead. Before that is reached it is hoped that those interested in their country's historic past will more universally recognize the place and the services of Jesse De Forest, the Walloon founder of the little pioneer settlement which has come to be the metropolis of the Western World.

[1] P. 51-53.

INDEX

----, Ariean 61
ALVA, 19 of 6 9
ARCHER, 5
AYLMER, Bishop of
  London 8
BEAUMONT, Anthonie 33
BEECKMAN, William 58
BLOCK, 31
BORNSTRA, Gertrude 55
BOUT, Willem Frederick 61
BOUWENSZ, Tyman 70
BRADFORD, 11-12 15 Gov
  10
BREWSTER, William 77
BRODHEAD, 30-31 42-43
  46
CALVERT, George 23 25
CAMPBELL, 8
CAMPION, 45
CARLETON, 25 45 Dudley
  22-23 45
CATOIR, 45
CHELLINGER, Capt 55
CHRISTIANSEN, 31
CLOUX, Marie Du 20 50
  Nicaise Du 20
CORNILLE, 45
DAMONT, 45
DAYNES, Gilles 33 Jehan
  33

DE CARPENTIER, 45
DE CRENNE, 45
DE CROY, 45
DE FOREEST, Gerrit 52
DE FOREST, 11 13-15 18-
  19 23 25 27-28 34 37-39
  45 53 58 61 69 75-76
  Anne 19-20 Gerard 20 49-
  52 Gerrit 52 Hendrick 20
  50-57 Henri 50 Henry 20
  Isaac 21 45 52-54 56-59
  62 72-74 J W 5 19 71 Jan
  57 Jean 19-20 Jehan 20
  Jesse 2 11 16-18 20 26 29-
  33 40-41 44 48-51 66 74
  77-80 Marie 20 Melchoir
  20 Mrs 60 Mrs Robert 12
  16 19 Rachel 33 48 50 56
  62 Sara 45 59 74
DE FREEST, Heindrick 55
DE LA MOT, 45
DE LAET, 31 Johannes 51
  John 30
DE LANCEY, Mrs Robert
  71
DE RIEMERS, 71
DE TROU, 45
DE TROUS, 75
DE VRIES, David 51
DENTON, John 57

DES FOREST, Jesse 27
DES FORESTS, Jean 20
  Jesse 20 33 Marie 20
DESCENDRE, Anthoine 33
  Anthonie 33
DIGAN, Bartheleme 33
DIGAND, Barthelemy 33
DOUILLERS, Abraham 33
DOZY, Charles M 77 79 Mr 78
DU CHESNE, Susanna 75
DU FOUR, 45
DU PON, 45
DU TRIEUX, 61 71 Philippe 45 75 80 Sara 45 74 Susanna 45 75
DUCHESNE, Susanna 45
EDMUNDSON, George 32
ELIZABETH, Queen of England 8
FOREST, Isaac Du 21 Jesse Du 20-21 Marie Du 20
FOXE, Mr 10
FREDERICSZ, Pieter 34
GASPAR, 45
GHISELIN, 45
GILLE, 45
GODEBON, Jehan 33
HALLAM, 9
HUDDE, Andries 55 Gertrude 55
HUDSON, Hendrik 30
JANSZ, Pieter 35

JOGUES, Father 59
JORIS, Adriaen 46
KIEFT, 66 68 Director 55 58-59 William 63
LA MONTAGNE, 40-41 45 48-51 53 55 58 63 65-67 76 Dr 48-49 54-55 63 75 Jan 59 Jean 76 Johannes 72 Mrs 61 Rachel 48 50 56 66
LA MONTAGNES, 71
LAMBERT, 45
LAUD, 12
LE MAIRE, 40
LE POU, 46
LE ROY, 45
LOUIS, King of 43
LOUIS XI, of France 17
LUCIFER, Adm 40
MAILLARD, Anne 19-20
MAIRE, Louis Le 33 36
MARTIN, 46
MASURE, Dominique 33
MATON, 46
MEY, 31 44 Cornelis 46 Cornelis Jacobsz 43 Cornelius 41
MICHAELIUS, Jonas 61
MINUIT, 70 78 Jean 69 Peter 69 77 Sara 69
MONTAGNE, 58 64 Jehan Mousnier 33 Jehan Mousnier De La 33

MONTAGNE (Cont.)
  Mousnier De La 25 Rachel 33
O'CALLAGHAN, 41 71
PARMA, Duchess of 22
RAPALYE, Caterina 45
  Catherine 45 Sarah De 45
  Simon De 45
ROBINSON, 11 13-14 John 10 77-79
SCHELLINGER, Jan 52
SCHEPEN, 72
SLOANE, Hans 32
STUYVESANT, 67 73 Gov 42 72 Peter 65
SWITS, Claesen 58
TEUNISSEN, Tobias 61
TILLOY, Sieur Du 20
TRICOT, Caterina 45
  Catherine 45
TRIEUX, Philippe Du 59 Sara Du 59
TROW, 75
TRUAX, 75
TURELL, 75
VAN HULST, Willem 69
VAN IMBROECH, Gysbert 66 Lysbet 66 Rachel 66
VAN IMBROECK, 71
VAN LAER, A J F 50
VAN RENSSELAER, 51 53 Kiliaen 50 52
VAN RYEN, Jan 48
VAN SICLEN, George W 77-78
VAN STAPELS, Gelyn 40 48
VAN TWILLER, 54
WASSENAER, 29-31 42-44 47
WHITGIFT, Archbishop of Canterbury 8
WILLEKENS, Adm 27
WILLIAM, of Orange 19
WILLIAM the Silent, 6
WOLFINGER, Leslie 13

www.ingramcontent.com/pod-product-compliance
Lightning Source LLC
Chambersburg PA
CBHW070321100426
42743CB00011B/2508